KIMBERLY'S FLIGHT

KIMBERLY'S FLIGHT

THE STORY OF
CAPTAIN KIMBERLY HAMPTON
AMERICA'S FIRST WOMAN COMBAT PILOT
KILLED IN BATTLE

BY ANNA SIMON & ANN HAMPTON

WITH A FOREWORD BY
LT. GENERAL WILLIAM B. CALDWELL, IV

CASEMATE

Philadelphia & Oxford

Published in the United States of America and Great Britain in 2012 by
CASEMATE PUBLISHERS
908 Darby Road, Havertown, PA 19083
and
10 Hythe Bridge Street, Oxford, OX1 2EW

ISBN 978-1-61200-102-9
Digital Edition: ISBN 978-1-61200-114-2

Cataloging-in-publication data is available from the Library of Congress
and the British Library.

10 9 8 7 6 5 4 3 2 1

Printed and bound in the United States of America.

For a complete list of Casemate titles please contact:

CASEMATE PUBLISHERS (US)
Telephone (610) 853-9131, Fax (610) 853-9146
E-mail: casemate@casematepublishing.com

CASEMATE PUBLISHERS (UK)
Telephone (01865) 241249, Fax (01865) 794449
E-mail: casemate-uk@casematepublishing.co.uk

"It is the Soldier" ©1970, 2012, used by permission of Charles M. Province,
U.S. Army, www.pattonhq.com

Photo, title page: Kimberly aboard a boat on a sightseeing visit to Alcatraz following
a college tennis trip over spring break during her senior year.

CONTENTS

MISSION OF THE OH-58D KIOWA WARRIOR:
Conduct armed reconnaissance, security, target acquisition and designation, command and control, light attack and defensive air combat missions in support of combat and contingency operations.

An OH-58D Kiowa Warrior helicopter provides close air support during operations in Iraq.
Staff Sergeant Jacob N. Bailey (USAF), defenseimagery.mil

TECHNICAL DATA:
   Crew: 2
   Max Gross Weight: 5,500 lbs (armed)
   Empty Weight: 3,289 lbs
   Height: 12 ft, 10.6 in
   Width: 6 ft, 5.4 in
   Length: 33 ft, 4 in
   Rotor Diameter: 35 ft
   Max Cruise Speed: 128 mph
   Range: 299 miles (sea level, no weapons, 10% reserve)
   Ceiling: 19,000 ft
   Armament: Air-to-air Stinger (ATAS) (2 round launcher); .50 caliber machine gun (500 rounds);
         HYDRA 70 (2.75 in) rockets (7-shot pod); HELLFIRE missiles (2-round launcher)

For every parent who has lost a child
And for those who serve and have served in our military services

••

In memory of
U.S. ARMY CAPTAIN KIMBERLY HAMPTON

August 18, 1976–January 2, 2004

First American female pilot
killed in action by the enemy

*"I am seeking, I am striving,
I am in it with all my heart."*

—Vincent Van Gogh

FOREWORD

By Lieutenant General William B. Caldwell, IV
Commander of the U.S. Army's 82nd Airborne Division,
May 2004–June 2006

I have so much respect for Capt. Kimberly Hampton, and speak about her courageous example so often, that people are always surprised when they discover that I never actually met her. They tell me that given the depth of my admiration for Kimberly, and the warmth with which I speak of her, they assume we must have been family friends or that we had served together multiple times.

The truth of how I came to know and admire Kimberly is, like so much in life, more complicated.

I took command of the 82nd Airborne Division on 28 May, 2004. Assuming the mantle of leadership for a division as steeped in prestige and tradition as the 82nd Airborne would be daunting under any circumstances, but it was even more challenging given that I was taking command while the division was in the midst of not one, but two simultaneous ground wars. I knew the 82nd had lost a number of paratroopers in combat in Afghanistan and Iraq. In order to get a better sense of the division's losses in the Global War on Terror, one of my first requests upon settling in as Commander was to view the book of the 82nd's fallen heroes.

As I pored over the list of paratroopers who had given their lives for their nation, one entry stood out:

CAPTAIN KIMBERLY HAMPTON, 2 JANUARY 2004,
FALLUJAH, IRAQ

A little research quickly confirmed my intuition that Kimberly was the first female soldier in the history of the 82nd Airborne to lose her life in combat. In addition, she was the first female pilot killed by enemy fire in Unites States history.

The significance of these facts goes far beyond mere trivia. It testifies to Kimberly's pioneer spirit, and it begins to illuminate the strength of her character.

It would be an understatement to describe the prevailing culture of the 82nd Airborne as macho. Not only does the act of jumping out of an airplane into the total darkness of night from a mere eight hundred feet above the ground require an aversion to risk most commonly found in testosterone-laden young males, but the physical rigors of jumping with more than one hundred pounds of combat equipment strapped to one's person challenges even the fittest male, not to mention typically lighter females. Consequently, women were not allowed to serve in the 82nd Airborne until 1979. Even today, these challenges remain large enough hurdles that the Division remains 90 to 95% male. This simple statistic says much about Captain Hampton's dedication and toughness.

It says even more about Kimberly that of all the military specialties available to her based upon her stellar career as a cadet at Presbyterian College, she chose combat attack aviation. While most aspiring helicopter pilots in the army, men and women alike, choose to serve as Blackhawk or Chinook pilots who ferry troops about the battlefield, Kimberly chose the far more dangerous path of becoming an OH-58 Kiowa pilot. This specialty meant that her mission was to actively seek out and engage the enemy, and it has only been open to women since the 1990s. She subsequently became one of the first female combat aviation commanders in the history of the 82nd Airborne. It was this decision which inevitably put her at the frontlines outside Fallujah, Iraq, on a fateful winter day.

Intrigued by her groundbreaking role, I began asking others in the division about Captain Hampton. Her peers shared with me the fact that she was absolutely loved by her troops. Her superior officers told me what a strong role model she provided for other paratroopers, and that she had the qualities and characteristics that marked her as a future general officer.

Command Sergeant Major "Wolf" Amacker, the 82nd's most senior non-commissioned officer, spoke of Kimberly's intensity, dedication, and compassion with pride and respect. He remembered that she was always smiling, and how contagious that smile was to everybody around her.

I have seen its reflection, but I wish I could have seen this smile in person.

Because of these tributes, I asked to meet Kimberly's parents, Ann and Dale Hampton. Seeing a child die young is an unnatural tragedy, and parents who lose a child in war react in a variety of ways. Understandably, some become withdrawn and have difficulty focusing on anything but their loss, even as the conflict rages on. Some become consumed by anger and rail against the causes and creeds their loved ones chose to serve. But Ann and Dale have followed a different path. They have internalized the values of selfless service and commitment. They talked proudly of Kimberly's dedication and why she chose a life of service. As we spoke, I began to realize where Kimberly drew her strength of character from all along and why she was such a perfect fit for the 82nd Airborne.

Ann and Dale are two of the most gracious and hospitable people I have ever been privileged to know. When Ann learned that I was deploying to Iraq myself in 2006, she sent me a bracelet with Kimberly's name and the date of her death.

I was honored to put it on, and I still wear that bracelet today.

As you will read in the pages to follow, Kimberly Hampton was a truly extraordinary young woman. She had choices. She could have followed any number of paths, and no doubt would have excelled in any challenge she set for herself. Her devotion to her country and her desire to make a meaningful contribution to her world led her to enroll in the Reserve Officer Training Corps program. As a result, she touched many lives, and many lives were shattered with her passing.

It is a tragedy of war that so many outstanding young leaders such as Capt. Kimberly Hampton are taken from us prematurely. It is a tribute to our nation that individuals such as Kimberly are willing to step forward to defend it with their lives.

In this sense, Capt. Kimberly Hampton was not an exception. But without a doubt, she was exceptional. My life will forever be changed because of her and what she represented. As one reads of the incredible accomplishments of Kimberly you will undoubtedly ask why? Why did someone who so cherished life, who gave so much to others, who served as such an incredible role model and literally could have done anything with her life; why did she serve and why did she, of all people, have to die? Her life is an inspiration to all of us, and through that she would want us to understand and appreciate her higher calling, that of serving our nation and serving others.

CHAPTER 1

FALLUJAH, IRAQ: JANUARY 2, 2004

S omewhere on a rooftop in Fallujah, a sniper was waiting, trying to blend in with the top of the building and hide from the two American helicopters flying above. His weapon was sighted on ground forces that had surrounded a riverside marketplace in the Iraqi city.

U.S. Army Capt. Kimberly Hampton and CWO (chief warrant officer) Donovan McCartney were flying low in an OH-58D Kiowa Warrior, a small, two-seat armed helicopter used for scouting missions. They knew the sniper was out there, somewhere. They scoured the urban landscape for any change in coloration, any hint of something out of place.

They knew they could take fire on this mission and never see the enemy take aim. Fortunately the enemy tended to miss far more often than hit its targets. The insurgents typically waited for the lead aircraft to pass and fired shots at the second aircraft from behind to avoid being seen from the air. Then they'd drop their weapons, blend into the general population on the streets and disappear.

Kimberly and Donovan realized they were stirring up a hornet's nest. Fallujah wasn't a nice place to be on the best of days. There were times when the infantry wouldn't even go into the town. Army intelligence had learned that black market gun merchants would be at the marketplace on the bank of the Euphrates River instead of the locals who usually sold food and textiles. Illegal weapons were laid out on the tables for sale in place of the usual bright-colored array of merchandise. American ground troops had surrounded the town so nobody could get out. The two helicopters overhead provided cover for American soldiers going in to seize the weapons.

Kimberly had been up before the Friday morning sun. They were supposed to take off at eight in the morning, but heavy ground fog delayed them for about an hour. It worked out all right though, because the ground troops they were covering were delayed as well.

As always, Kimberly had taken her long curly blonde hair out of the tight bun typically worn by women in the military and pulled it into a ponytail just before getting into the cockpit. The helmet wouldn't fit over her bun. She was commander of Delta Troop, 1st Squadron, 17th Cavalry, referred to as the Darkhorses, of the 82nd Airborne Division. She had such presence that Donovan tended to forget she was a female until he saw her hair down. When she finished flying, Kimberly always paused beside the aircraft and put her hair back up in the bun before moving on. She was the first female commander of this cavalry unit, but first and foremost she was a soldier and wanted to be recognized as such.

Donovan liked to fly with Kimberly. On missions, it was all business. Donovan usually flew the aircraft, as he did this day, while Kimberly ran the mission. It was a different story while they flew to and from missions. They'd sing old rock and roll songs to pass the time and sometimes Kimberly would take the controls. She could make the aircraft dance. She loved to fly, and she loved to lead her troops. As a commander she had the privilege of doing both and was confident and happy in her work. She was a natural leader and had complete respect from her troops without ever raising her voice.

Above Fallujah that day, they flew as they usually did, in teams of two helicopters, each team taking its turn in the air while the other refueled and rested. Kimberly and Donovan had completed their first flight, took a refueling break and were nearing the end of their second bag of gas, about 12:20 PM, when they felt an explosion. They were less than a hundred feet above the ground and starting on another inbound run toward the city.

"What was that?" asked Kimberly, who was directing the mission.

"I don't know," answered Donovan, who was at the controls feverishly trying to keep the spinning aircraft upright.

The Kiowa Warrior was traveling at about 90 knots, about 103 mph, and took a couple of seconds to reach the ground. There was no panic in the cockpit. There was no time to be afraid or even realize what had happened.

A heat-seeking surface-to-air missile had gone into the exhaust system of the helicopter and knocked off the tail boom. It was a fairly sophisticated weapon compared to what typical Iraqi insurgents had.

The aircraft spiraled downward and smashed into a brick wall surrounding a date and apple orchard. It hit the wall nose down on the pilot's side, crushing the nose and dashboard in on them. Donovan lost consciousness. The helicopter rolled up under some trees. The infantry had to use a truck to pull the aircraft apart to get to them.

When Donovan came to, he was being pulled out of the aircraft by a big infantry soldier who told Donovan he saw the rocket-like missile fly into the air and hit them.

Kimberly was dead. She died instantly of injuries to her head and chest with little bleeding. That's when the miracles began.

Kimberly, age six.

CHAPTER 2

ANN HAMPTON:
EASLEY, SOUTH CAROLINA, 1982

K imberly and our neighbor Sam Hinkie ran through the woods behind our adjoining back-to-back suburban homes and slid to the ground behind the Hinkies' woodpile. Bits of grass and red Carolina clay stained the knees of their pants as they crawled around the woodpile, dragging their plastic guns behind them. They were silent for a moment as the imaginary enemy passed. Then they scrambled across the yard on their bellies and climbed the nine steps to their hideout, a steep-roofed little playhouse that Sam's mother, Sarita, had spotted while shopping one day. It sat up above the ground like a hunter's tree stand, supported by long wooden legs. Army was their favorite game. They loved to wear Sam's father's old camouflage fatigues. One would wear the top and the other wore the bottoms. The arms and legs were long enough to trip over, but Kimberly and Sam didn't care.

It was time to call Kimberly in to clean up for supper, but Sarita hadn't called for Sam yet, so I decided to give them a little more time outside. Jack, our tri-colored collie, wagged his tail furiously as the children clambered back down the playhouse steps. Sarita waved Sam inside and Kimberly rolled in the grass with Jack and then laid her head on the dog's side, using him like a pillow. He licked at her blonde curls and put his paw across her.

The afternoon sun filtered through the trees at a slant. I paused at the window a moment more, freezing the picture of Kimberly and the dog piled up together in my mind before I disturbed them. I had waited so long for this child and now Kimberly was about to start first grade. Time was slipping by too fast.

I asked Dale out on our first date, a church hayride in 1960. We became high school sweethearts and dreamed of a family after we married, but no children came. A decade later we talked to doctors, considered adoption and Dale underwent surgery, but after twelve years of marriage our hopes had faded.

Then I went to my doctor with some female problems. In the middle of the exam, he told the nurse, "Break out the champagne!"

I didn't understand at first . . . then it hit me: I was pregnant!

I called Dale and was so overcome with emotion that all I could do was cry. Poor Dale was scared to death. He couldn't understand a word I said. Every time I tried to speak, more sobs came out. I finally calmed down and he realized what I was trying to say.

Kimberly came by C-section on August 18, 1976. My sister Louise and one of my friends tried to keep Dale calm in the hospital waiting room. I

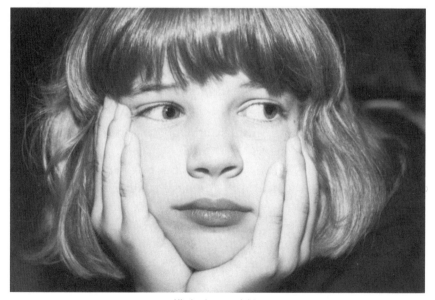

Kimberly, age eight.

wasn't there to see Dale hold Kimberly for the first time. Hospitals were different back then. But Louise told me all about it. When the doctor placed Kimberly in Dale's arms, all he could do was walk around in disbelief, repeating "I can't believe it! I can't believe it!" over and over again.

A few hours later, Dale and I walked from my hospital room to the nursery window and looked in. One of the nurses had pulled Kimberly's crib off to the side and was reading to her. Kimberly was born with a thick head of hair and was the only girl in the hospital nursery. I was sure that the nurse felt like I did . . . that Kimberly was the most beautiful baby there. My heart overflowed with joy. Kimberly was a miracle, a very special gift, and I had no doubt this baby came from God.

As a toddler, Kimberly seemed to fall down more often than other children. I was concerned and talked to the pediatrician about it.

"She'll probably never be able to run without falling," she told me and recommended that I buy her some special corrective shoes.

I was heartbroken. I immediately bought the shoes for Kimberly: a pair of heavy white lace-up shoes with built up soles and heels. She fell less often, but she stumbled a lot in the clunky shoes. It hurt to watch her struggle, and I took her to an orthopedic specialist for a second opinion.

"Throw the shoes in the trash and let Kimberly wear tennis shoes

Kimberly, eight, and her beloved grandmother, Ma-Ma, at eighty.

or sandals or go barefoot," the specialist told me.

But his diagnosis was disturbing as well. He wasn't worried about Kimberly's feet. He was concerned about her back.

A few years later when she was in elementary school Kimberly was diagnosed with scoliosis, an abnormal curvature of the spine. I also have scoliosis, which tends to run in families, although I didn't know it then. It was only years later that I was diagnosed. After talking with the specialist I happily tossed the heavy shoes in the trash. Even at that early age Kimberly was such a determined child, and before long she was running and playing like any other child, without falling down.

My whole family doted on Kimberly. Everyone treated her like a little princess. She grew up surrounded by love and returned it tenfold with sweet hugs and kisses and a burning desire to please. My oldest sister, Frances, had three sons. Louise and my other sister Martha had no children. Kimberly was my mother's only granddaughter, and she was much younger than Frances's three boys. My mother always called her the baby or Babe, and Kimberly called her Ma-Ma.

Kimberly and my mother shared a special relationship. I'd watched my mother struggle with loneliness for four years after my father died. To say I'd worried about her would be an understatement. Kimberly's arrival gave her a new lease on life. The sun came out and the clouds of loneliness lifted.

Ma-Ma kept Kimberly during the day when Dale and I were at work and became a central figure in Kimberly's life. They spent winter afternoons on the sofa laughing at *I Love Lucy* and *Mayberry RFD* reruns. They'd spend hours and hours just sitting there, and Kimberly was perfectly content. In the spring, summer and fall, they'd spend those countless hours in Ma-Ma's flower and vegetable gardens. Kimberly learned to plant seeds, pull weeds and help with the harvest. She loved to eat right out of the garden, and she always loved vegetables, salads and greens. She especially loved to pluck the sweet, golden-brown figs from Ma-Ma's tree and pop them straight into her mouth.

I think much of Kimberly's love for the natural world was rooted in the time spent in Ma-Ma's garden, and I believe Kimberly's unpretentious and nurturing nature sprang from the simple joys they shared.

Nothing in the world, not even my kisses, had the same magical medicinal properties as Ma-Ma's homemade macaroni and cheese. I don't think that even I realized the depth of their bond until after my mother's death.

It just killed Kimberly when we sold Ma-Ma's house.

"I spent half of my childhood in that house," she said.

"Honey, why didn't you tell us?" I asked her.

I don't know how we would have done it, but we would have found some way to buy it, had we realized how much it meant to Kimberly.

Kimberly always was very sentimental. Although she reveled in traveling the world as an adult, she relied on her home and family to be her anchors and provide stability in a world that, especially after the terrorist attacks of 2001, was changing fast.

We redid Kimberly's bedroom while she was in Korea. It was a big room, and we changed out the little girl stuff for more mature décor. I thought she'd be thrilled. I was wrong.

"It's not my room anymore," she said when she came home and saw it.

"Kimberly, you've been gone for years."

"I don't care," she responded."

As a soldier she thrived on excitement and adventure, but she wanted everything at home to always remain the same. I should have known. Even as a child Kimberly pushed herself to the front lines of life both in the classroom and on the tennis court, but home was a refuge where she could retreat into a love-filled cocoon, like a queen amid admiring subjects, and recharge for the next challenge ahead.

That cocoon of love was most evident at Christmas, when everyone gathered at our house to see Kimberly open her gifts. She meticulously unwrapped each package without tearing the paper and then heaped hugs, kisses, and thanks on the benefactor before opening the next box. One of my most precious treasures is a little red and green construction paper-covered book she made in fourth grade filled with her stories about Christmas:

When mother walks down our stairs and announces I am awake, my aunts, uncles, and other relatives get their cameras ready. As soon as I walk down the stairs my eyes are almost blinded because of the sudden flash of cameras. I enjoy Christmas at my house and hope it will never change.

—Kimberly, from her fourth grade Christmas book

Kimberly was in elementary school when she and Sam discovered tennis. They'd hit balls against the side of our brick house for hours, using Sam's father's racquetball racquet and Dale's old wooden tennis racquet. She developed a fairly accurate swing early to avoid hitting any windows, but one day a ball got away. It crashed through her second floor bedroom window. She was devastated. Kimberly didn't like making mistakes. I often told her that she was her own worst critic, and she could be hard on herself. That was to be a lifelong trait.

I'll always remember the day that Kimberly, who was usually meek and calm, came home from school spitting fire after her teacher told her she was too much of a perfectionist.

"I'm not trying to be a perfectionist," she said, pursing her lips with frustration.

The teacher just doesn't understand, she said.

"Here I am trying to do my best, and she's telling me to lighten up!"

Kimberly was driven by achievement, not perfection. She wanted to please us and make us proud, but it was more than that. A desire to excel was embedded in her personality. Kimberly lived life like a game of tennis. She wanted each serve to be better than the last. She wanted to return every ball and surmount every challenge. She refueled on victory and saw defeat as only a temporary setback. She knew the difference between being good and being great, and she refused to settle for just being good.

That was the standard she set for herself in her schoolwork, with her tennis, and later, in her career.

Her superiors in the military later told us how hard she worked to do everything the right way and please them.

"I don't want them coming to me telling me I didn't do it right," she'd say. Whatever she did, she gave it her best. For Kimberly, there was no other way.

We watched Kimberly develop her backyard tennis swing, and one day Dale took her to the city tennis courts at Easley's Pope Field. They volleyed the ball back and forth across the net and Dale was amazed at her skill and coordination at such a young age.

"Do you want to take tennis lessons?"

"Sure," she said.

Kimberly had found her passion. We started with Darelyn Holliday, an Easley tennis instructor with a reputation for giving young students a good foundation. Tennis opened a whole new world for Kimberly and released her competitive spirit. Sam went along with Dale and me to watch her play in novice tournaments and we cheered her on from the sidelines, a trio of faithful fans. Her skills steadily improved, and before long, she was accepted in a highly respected tournament program in nearby Belton and began to face stiffer competition.

Even as a preteen, Kimberly was serious about her game. She was disciplined and cut no corners in training. She was fiery and competitive and focused. It was usually easier to please the coach than herself. She was a good sport toward her opponents, but she was very hard on herself if she lost. Some of the girls she played against at country clubs around the state cried at losses or complained about the officiating—some threw racquets. Kimberly never did. She couldn't stand that sort of misbehavior and it fueled her to play even harder against her more tantrum-prone opponents.

Some of the girls seemed to care as much about their hair or wardrobe as the match, and that always puzzled Kimberly. While she was always properly attired and well-groomed she was unconcerned about her appearance. She just wanted to win.

Kimberly's demeanor on the court was always the same. She played with constant focus whether she was winning or losing. But occasionally, when she knew she was doing well, she'd sneak a look at us and wink.

"She can be as good as she wants to be," her new coach, Chuck Waldron, told us one day as we watched her play.

I worried about how harsh she was on herself when she lost, but he was unconcerned. Losing builds character, he said. It's what inspires her to be better.

Off the court, Kimberly was absorbed by the world tennis scene. She followed the careers of Steffi Graf and other top tennis stars closely. She admired their work ethic and the sacrifices they made to rise above the competition. They were her role models.

SAM HINKIE—
Kimberly and I talked a lot about what it took to get to the top, how hard

people had to work and how even when you got to the top, you had to keep working.

"You can let up when you get to the top," I tried to tell her, but she just laughed.

"When you get to the top you have to work even harder to stay there," she retorted.

Kimberly played on the boys' tennis team at Easley Junior High because the school didn't have a girls' team yet. She took particular joy in winning when she played against boys.

A girls' team was formed when Kimberly was in ninth grade and she quickly emerged as the star player. She and Alicia Limbaugh, friends since elementary school, often warmed up together before matches and occasionally played doubles as partners. Alicia's outgoing personality was a contrast to Kimberly's quieter, serious demeanor and Alicia helped Kimberly shed her shyness by encouraging her to get involved in student government and other activities.

They served together on the Easley High Student Council and Kimberly was elected secretary in her junior year. Alicia and other friends suggested that she run for student body president, but Kimberly didn't want the attention and she didn't think she could win. Her friends coaxed and cajoled until she gave in. I don't know if she quite believed it yet when she called from school to tell me she had won the election.

When Easley High started a Naval Junior ROTC program during Kimberly's senior year, her instructor, Capt. Jim Franklin, completely replaced all of her former role models, the international tennis stars she'd admired and tried to emulate. His dedication, professionalism, passion for his job, and compassion for his students inspired her and set an example that she held as a standard for the remainder of her life. Kimberly, who had loved scrambling in the dirt and playing army with Sam, was in her element in ROTC, and Captain Franklin nurtured her emerging leadership abilities. She was selected as the battalion commander and began to seriously consider a military career.

Kimberly told her Uncle Bob, Louise's husband, what she was thinking. Bob loved to fly and Kimberly shared his enthusiasm. He told her, much to my chagrin, that she'd fly airplanes one day. I was proud of her accomplishments in ROTC, but I secretly hoped she would become an English teacher and tennis coach and stay closer to home.

I was glad to see that Kimberly's new ROTC activities had not hampered her drive on the courts. Kimberly was Easley High's top seed and her feisty determination had caught the eye of Presbyterian College tennis coach Donna Arnold. Donna liked Kimberly's powerful serve and the way she charged the net the moment the ball left her racquet. Because she was recruiting, Donna had to keep her eye on Kimberly from a distance, but we could tell Donna was watching.

Kimberly tended to show off a bit when Donna was around, and the interest was flattering, but Kimberly loved ROTC as much as tennis. She found a way to do both.

Senator Fritz Hollings nominated Kimberly for West Point. Kimberly was beside herself with excitement when a telegram confirmed her nomination.

Kimberly was going to play tennis at West Point.

Kimberly's graduation was a proud day. She graduated with honors and gave the invocation at commencement. The girls wore white graduation gowns and the boys wore green, the Easley High colors, and sunlight filled the sky. It was a picture perfect, except for a bittersweet sadness at the prospect of parting.

My, my, my—so many memories . . . Why do we have to grow up? We've had fun—
I'm sure that when I see you again we'll act just as childish and carefree as we used to.
—Kimberly's message in her friend Katherine Lathem's
1994 Green & White senior yearbook.

Kimberly and her grandparents Bill and Lucille Hampton.

CHAPTER 3

A SECOND CHANCE

K imberly cried when we left her at West Point in late June. We were stunned. Kimberly rarely cried. Even when Jack, our beloved collie, was killed by a car we saw no tears. We knew she had to cry, but she couldn't even talk about it. She put pictures of Jack all over the house, and we knew she was grieving, but she was always stoic. Instead of talking about Jack's death, she wrote a poem about it. That was her way. She always seemed to find it easier to express her feelings on paper than verbally.

Kimberly had been at West Point's Beast Barracks for new cadets for two days when she called and said she wanted to come home.

"I really think I want to have a life during my college career," she told us. "As much as I am in awe of this place, I really feel like I want to go back to school someplace near home."

West Point called, too.

"She's doing great. Everything she does is just super. She does everything we ask her to do and more, but she says she doesn't want to be here. Help us out."

Give her time, she'll come around, they said. They really tried to convince her to stay. She was their top tennis recruit. But we allowed Kimberly to make her own choice, and in retrospect, I'm glad we did.

After two weeks at the Military Academy, Kimberly came home.

She always had the utmost respect for anyone who went to West Point and stayed, but she didn't want that much structure in her life, and she wanted to be closer to home.

In the fall, Kimberly entered Furman University, in Greenville, about half an hour from home. She had been accepted there before she went to West Point, and first semester she played on Furman's respected Division I tennis team. But the college life she envisioned continued to elude her.

Kimberly's freshman year was a traumatic time for her. She'd come home from West Point; she had given up a free four-year education, and she felt like she had let everyone down.

I also wondered whether an opportunity had been lost, although I never voiced the question to Kimberly. One day I talked about it with Mike O'Kane, a friend at work and retired army full colonel.

"Focus on the fact that she had what it took to get there," he said.

If Kimberly decided on a military career, it really wouldn't matter if she graduated from West Point or another school, he said.

"You're really judged on what you're doing on the battlefield, your training and how you're leading your troops."

I knew Kimberly would be a strong leader if she chose that route. The conversation made me feel better about her decision. But Kimberly was still beating herself up over it, and nothing Dale or I told her seemed to ease her burden.

It wasn't until she came home at Christmas and went over to the high school to visit her former ROTC instructor, U.S. Navy Capt. Jim Franklin, that she reached a turning point. He was her mentor, her friend, and her hero. In Kimberly's eyes, he was the epitome of a military officer and she valued his advice.

"It's ok. I'm not disappointed in you. No one is disappointed in you," he told her.

She hated to disappoint anybody. One thing that drove her was to please. She wanted to make her parents, her friends, everybody proud and happy.

But Kimberly wasn't happy. The rigors of a Division I tennis program and her college studies were demanding, and there was no time for ROTC, but Kimberly wanted to be in ROTC and was beginning to seriously consider a military career.

Kimberly with Easley High School ROTC instructor, U.S. Navy Capt. Jim Franklin, a mentor, role model, and friend who she considered to be the epitome of a military officer.

Captain Franklin encouraged Kimberly to apply for a three-year army ROTC scholarship, if that's what she wanted to do.

It was.

Kimberly was laughing and crying at the same time the day she called to tell me that she'd gotten the ROTC scholarship. She was absolutely giddy.

"Mom, I've been given a second chance. Very few people get this in life."

She didn't know it, but her real second chance was yet to come.

At Presbyterian College, which was a bit farther away in Clinton, South Carolina, tennis coach Donna Arnold, who had been so interested in Kimberly during high school, got word that Kimberly wasn't totally happy at Furman. She jumped at another opportunity to recruit Kimberly. This was a second chance for Donna, too.

Donna enlisted the help of Lt. Col. Kirk Thomas, who headed Presbyterian's ROTC program. The timing was perfect. Presbyterian College had just approved an ROTC scholarship incentive, and Thomas was able to put together a package that trumped Furman's offer.

Thomas was new at Presbyterian and had inherited a troubled program. It wasn't meeting its quota of graduating officers, and the army gave notice that the program would be closed. South Carolina's senior Senator Strom Thurmond pressured the army to wait and give the new PMS (professor of military science, the title of the army officer in charge of a college's

ROTC program) a chance. Thomas offered Kimberly a full scholarship. He desperately needed enthusiastic student leaders interested in military careers if he was to save one of the nation's oldest ROTC programs. The college approved scholarships to cover the gap between the ROTC scholarship and the full cost of college.

After the first semester, I realized that I really wanted to be in the military, I really wanted to play college tennis and I really wanted to do well in school. I applied for a three year ROTC scholarship and got it. At the same time, I communicated with the tennis coach at PC and she said she would welcome me on the team if I transferred. I knew the tennis demands (Div. II) and the classroom demands wouldn't be as tough at PC. In addition, the PC ROTC alumni pick up the tab for the difference between the Army ROTC "full" (not really) scholarship and the cost of tuition, room, and board. Furman said they would "see what they could do" about funding the difference (about $6,000 a year). That helped me make up my mind and I decided to transfer after my freshman year. That was probably the best decision I've ever made."

—e-mail from Kimberly in Afghanistan, November 26, 2002, to Rick Simmons, also in Afghanistan

Kimberly finally found the college life she'd dreamed of on the tree-

Kimberly relaxes between matches during a Presbyterian College tennis tournament. *Courtesy of "Daddy Coach" Harold Arnold, Coach Donna Arnold's father*

shaded Presbyterian College campus of about twelve hundred students. The school was about an hour from Easley, and like Furman, it was an easy drive. Kimberly majored in English, played tennis and was in ROTC. She was instantly happy on the small campus in a small town not unlike Easley.

Lush grassy plazas divided rows of traditional red brick and white columned buildings on the long, narrow campus. The entire campus is only about two city blocks wide but it's a mile in length from the administrative buildings just off the main street to the athletic fields on the back side of the campus. The tennis courts are about midway across the length of the campus, not far from the short flight of concrete steps down to the ROTC offices and classrooms in the basement of one of the brick buildings. Kimberly spent a lot of time in both places.

KATHERINE LATHEM, Kimberly's classmate and friend since elementary school and at Presbyterian College—

She made friends right away, excelled with her grades and rose to the top just like she always did. You wouldn't know just seeing her around campus that she was the tennis champ, the smart one, the ROTC person and that kind of thing. She didn't act it. She was very humble with her talents.

Kimberly gives her father Dale a hug after a Presbyterian College tennis match.

Kimberly's alarm went off at 5:30 AM three days a week when she had PT (physical training) with the other ROTC cadets. She seemed to breeze through her classes, and made mostly A's, but we knew that was because she did the work. She made it look easy, but Kimberly had developed good discipline, organizational skills, and study habits early in life. Homework was part of what it took to get to the top and stay there, and that was always Kimberly's goal.

After classes, Kimberly had tennis practice until about 6 PM. At the end of practice, the team raced to the dining hall before it closed. There was just enough time for a quick shower after supper before study hall, which was required for the first-year players: freshmen and transfer students like Kimberly. Her schedule was packed but she never appeared to be stressed. She stayed up all night writing papers and still brimmed with energy at early morning PT. She never let her friends see her juggling act, but Dale and I knew she worked hard at everything she did. Sometimes she came home to rest and recharge, and we just let her sleep.

Kimberly tennis teammates called her Kimbo. She was a coach's dream, Donna said: serious and ready to work hard with an ever-present smile that exuded confidence. She went into her matches fully believing even before the first serve hit the air that she would win.

Kimberly won every singles match in conference play through her college career at Presbyterian. She was captain of the tennis team during her junior and senior years and was named South Atlantic Conference Player of the year as a junior. Kelli Kirkland, a friend and tennis teammate at Presbyterian, remembered, "Her confidence instilled confidence in us." Dean's-list grades earned Kimbo NCAA Division II Academic All-America honors that year as well.

Kimberly never shied away from a challenge, and spurred a bit of a battle of the sexes with her male ROTC counterparts, although Lieutenant Colonel Thomas wasn't sure whether she was aware of her influence because she was always so focused on the task at hand. Thomas was amused when Kimberly was the first of the ROTC cadets to go off the rappelling tower. The men had to follow after that, although he could tell some of them were scared to death.

Kimberly's enthusiasm was an asset for the ROTC program that Thomas did manage to save. There were few women in the program when

Kimberly entered, and having someone of her caliber was a big plus in recruiting other women, he said.

Although she was heavily involved in tennis and a nationally ranked player, she willingly put in the extra after-hours work required by ROTC to prepare to become an army officer, and she instinctively knew how to lead and motivate others without overshadowing them

"She would reach down and try to pull people up instead of putting people down because they didn't have the qualities she had," said Cathy Whitman, the human resource assistant for the ROTC program and a substitute mother for the cadets. "When Kimberly walked into a room, she came right into your heart. If you could ever have the perfect cadet, she was the perfect cadet."

About the only thing Kimberly couldn't do was the "quick feet ladder," a training exercise Donna used to help players with their foot work. "It was like she had three feet," Donna said. Others also struggled with the ladder, but Kimberly was the only one they laughed at, because they'd never seen her stumble. And she laughed with them.

But no one laughed when Kimberly walked onto the tennis court. She was intense and a fierce competitor. Her forehand was explosive and her serve was full of power. No one could touch her once she was in the zone.

"Come on, Kimberly," her friend Kelli would shout from the sidelines watching. "Come ON!"

"That's what I'm talking about!" Dale would chime in after a good swing.

Although Kimberly won every singles match in conference play, there were losses outside of the conference schedule. Presbyterian played some of the top teams in the nation over spring break and at nationals at the end of the school year, and Kimberly loved the challenge.

"She played some of her best tennis in these contests," Donna said. Even when she lost to top level players, Kimberly "never got blown off the court. She knew when she came off the court that she'd given them a match."

Kimberly was humble about her wins and always showed respect for the other players. But when she lost she was quiet. Very quiet.

"It was almost like her heart broke," Kelli said.

But Kimberly never talked about it. Sometimes she needed a little time alone with Donna before she came off the court. Sometimes she'd shed a tear or two, but only when she was alone with her teammates, Donna, or Dale and me.

Kimberly watched her teammates play with the same intense focus she had on the court, exuding a silent leadership that pushed them harder than one of her serves.

She rarely hollered or cheered, but just when Kelli needed a boost, she'd hear Kimberly's low, calm voice:

"Here we go Kel, let's go Kel."

Dale always traveled with the team and I did when I could. We were like a big, laughing, traveling family on the road, booking tables for fifty at the most interesting restaurants we could find and enjoying local attractions along the way.

Kimberly often slept on the van, exhausted from her non-stop days on campus. The front passenger seat was her domain, slightly apart from the excited chatter and a place to close her eyes and recharge. Sometimes she was out before the engine started and rarely woke until they reached their destination. Then she'd put on her headphones and listen to music and focus on the match.

Nothing stopped her. She sprained her ankle during a singles match in Savannah, soaked it in a bucket of ice slush, taped it up and went back out on the court and won. When she had the flu, she rode to the tournament with Dale and me, so she could lie down in the car and sleep. When we got to the match, she threw up and then she went out on the court and played.

The summer after her sophomore year, Kimberly shared an apartment with Darah Huffman, a basketball player who was in ROTC with Kimberly. It was one of the few times in her life that Kimberly slowed her pace. They each had one morning class and spent the rest as they pleased. They barbecued outdoors, worked out, ran, and sunbathed on the intramural fields while they studied. Kimberly lived on fruit and healthy foods, and Darah teased her for being so disciplined about her health and her studies.

"I don't know if I'd have made it through college without her," Darah later said. "She made me study all the time. She was even fun to study with. She was positive in every kind of way."

Kimberly and Darah drove to Charlotte for a James Taylor concert. They flew to Jacksonville, Florida, to spend the Fourth of July holiday with Darah's family. Kimberly took Darah to Table Rock State Park, in the Blue Ridge Mountains north of Easley, and Darah took Kimberly to her family's mountain house near Highlands, N.C., for whitewater rafting.

The water was like ice even in summer, Darah recalled:

> The sides of the river were beautiful and wild, a mix of green and rock. As the raft tossed and turned through a long waterfall-like run of rapids, we both fell out. The water rushed by and we choked for air at the mercy of the current until other rafters threw ropes to us and pulled us to safety.

Afterward they laughed, and the tale turned into legend.

When fall semester started, Kimberly resumed her busy lifestyle, but she had a little more freedom. Now in their second year on the tennis team, Kelli and Kimberly were free of the nightly study hall requirement and often stayed on the courts after tennis practice hitting balls together into the night. Then they'd hop into Kimberly's gold Honda, open the sunroof wide, crank up the cassette player and sing along with the Indigo Girls or other '80's music and go off campus for dinner. They liked El Jalisco, a Mexican restaurant, and Whitefields, a popular local hamburger and ice cream shop. Sometimes they'd drive all the way to Greenville to Pete's Drive-In for Oreo milkshakes.

Kimberly wanted people to see her as tough. But beneath her confident ROTC and tennis team captain exterior, she was a sensitive and intensely private person. Kimberly was unselfish, a great listener, and a caring friend, Kelli said.

Kimberly struggled over her career decision. She was pulled in three different directions. She couldn't decide whether she wanted to be a teacher and tennis coach, have a military career, or go into law. She agonized over her choices, and then, in her junior year, Kimberly made her commitment to serve in the army.

I went back to my friend Colonel O'Kane and asked if he would be willing to talk with Kimberly about what to expect from an army career. He took Kimberly to lunch at the Commerce Club in Greenville one day. It was the summer before senior year, and Kimberly was leaving soon to go to ROTC Advance Camp at Ft. Lewis, Washington.

"I was fascinated by her perseverance, and tenacity of purpose and resolve. She was really focused like a laser beam on what she wanted to do," Colonel O'Kane said.

She wanted to be an aviator and a paratrooper, and Colonel O'Kane spent a good part of the two-hour lunch trying to talk her out of it. It was obvious that she had what it takes to be successful, but because she was a woman, he wasn't sure she'd have the opportunities to advance.

"I don't know if there's a glass ceiling, but my perception is that women have to work harder than men to get ahead in the army," he told her.

Kimberly wasn't deterred.

"It seems you're determined," Colonel O'Kane told her and pulled a silver eagle pin he wore as a colonel from his pocket and showed it to her.

"Look at the thousands of feathers on that eagle. Each feather represents thousands and thousands of soldiers," he said, and talked about the responsibility she would bear for many American lives as she advanced through the ranks.

He handed her the pin and told her that all he asked was that if she did enjoy a successful army career that she one day pass the pin on to another.

"Big tears came into her eyes, and mine too, and she said, 'I will do that.'"

The time Kimberly spent at Ft. Lewis that summer reaffirmed her commitment to the army and we could see her enthusiasm in her notes home.

I'm training to be the best Army officer I can be. I'll settle for nothing less than the best—my best. . . . The U.S. needs good, solid troops in the "hot spots". That's where I want to be. I don't think I can serve in fear of being sent to war. Of course we want to avoid war, but conflicts are inevitable. America's best should be devoted to serving in those conflicts—without fear and without hesitation. I'm sure there are people who no longer support the U.S. military or the government, but whether I agree with what we do or not, I have a duty and an obligation to serve. I may be one of the few people who still consider it a privilege and an honor to serve my country.

—June 20, 1997 letter from Kimberly to Dale and Ann

Her decision to join the army was made, but Kimberly still had to decide what branch she wanted to serve in. She took the Alternate Flight Aptitude Selection Test required for anyone interested in flying in April of 1997, before going to Ft. Lewis. She took her flight physical at Advance Camp, but also was interested in field artillery and legal work with the judge advocate general corps. When she got back to school in the fall, she talked about her options with Lt. Col. Larry Mulhall, the new military science professor who headed the ROTC program after Lieutenant Colonel Thomas left in Kimberly's senior year.

Kimberly was the ROTC battalion commander of Presbyterian's Scottish Highlander Battalion during her senior year. Lieutenant Colonel Thomas had recommended Kimberly for the battalion command when he turned his position over to Lieutenant Colonel Mulhall. There were three other good prospects, but Lieutenant Colonel Mulhall could see that Kimberly stood out.

"She had the instincts of an army captain," he said.

She used her reassuring, low Southern voice to her advantage and knew how to push people forward without overshadowing them. She moved easily among various groups of people and had a respectful manner and a mature presence about her. Out in the field, all the other cadets would be in rumpled clothing pulled from their rucksacks, but Kimberly would have on a fresh uniform and look like she'd just left home.

Lieutenant Colonel Mulhall knew that Kimberly had the ability to go far, but he feared her future would be limited in field artillery. At that time certain combat slots were for males only. And she'd be too far from the action to be happy in the adjutant general corps, he said.

Kimberly wanted to fly and was confident she could handle the academic side of flight school, but she'd never flown and feared competing with people from aviation families who had flying in their blood.

"It's a lot like tennis," Lieutenant Colonel Mulhall told her. Flying a helicopter "is hand and eye coordination."

With his encouragement, Kimberly listed aviation as her first choice when she filled out her request.

Kimberly's e-mails and letters home over the summer at Ft. Lewis were filled with excitement over field artillery exercises, so I was startled when Kimberly announced that she wanted to fly. Kimberly planned the timing well. She made her announcement in a restaurant after a tennis match with the whole team, so there wasn't much I could say. I didn't want my only child in harm's way, but I was proud Kimberly was pursuing lofty goals. I just wanted to hug her and keep her close, but I loved Kimberly enough to let her fly.

Kimberly anxiously awaited word from Army Aviation. She was nervous about the flight-school physical. Her old scoliosis showed up on a high school physical, but not at West Point. It cropped up on the ROTC physical at Presbyterian, and she'd entered the program on a medical waiver.

Presbyterian College tennis Coach Donna Arnold gives Kimberly advice
during her last tennis match on the college's team.

Kimberly was beside herself when her flight-school acceptance arrived. She couldn't wait to get to Ft. Rucker, the home of army aviation.

"Are you afraid to die in war?" Darah asked Kimberly one day.

"No," Kimberly replied. "If I did, to die for your country would be the most honorable thing to do."

After Kelli and Kimberly watched the movie *Courage Under Fire* starring Meg Ryan as a female helicopter pilot, Kelli looked at Kimberly with tears in her eyes.

"Is this what you are going to do?" Kelli asked. "You could die."

Kimberly just said yes, that's what she's going to do, fly helicopters. She never talked about dying.

In May 1998, Kimberly graduated from Presbyterian College with honors, but missed commencement to play her last college match at the NCAA Division II nationals in Springfield, Missouri, for the top sixteen teams nationally in the division. Each of Kimberly's three years at Presbyterian College, the team had been one of sixteen selected to compete. I drank in every move of Kimberly's last game with a lump in my throat. She gave her pro circuit-caliber opponent a good game, but lost. The entire team embraced in a teary-eyed hug when it was over, and Donna gave her a ball from the match.

Kimberly receives the Wysor Saber, an honor awarded to the top Presbyterian College ROTC cadet.

Kimberly finished her tennis career ranked twenty-eighth nationally in singles and eighteenth in doubles, with a 27–0 singles record in the South Atlantic Conference. She held conference singles titles in 1997 and 1998 and was the SAC Female Athlete of the Year in 1998. And on the military side she received the Wysor Saber, which is awarded to the top ROTC cadet.

Kimberly was commissioned a second lieutenant in the U.S. Army in a private ceremony with family and friends at the college. Like graduation, the scheduled ROTC commissioning also took place while she was away at the NCAA Division II national tournament, so the private ceremony was arranged. After she was commissioned, she gave a little impromptu speech thanking us all for our support.

Everyone there had played a part in Kimberly's life. Without calling them by name, she found a way to let each one know that she was thanking them, and as always, she had special thanks for Dale and me. Her commissioning was a proud day for all of us, and I had tears in my eyes. Dressed in her uniform, with her hair neatly pulled back in a bun, she seemed to have transformed overnight and was no longer a college student but a professional military officer. We knew then that our little girl belonged to Uncle Sam. Our commissioning gift to her was a small pair of diamond earrings, which fit the size and criteria to wear with her Class A dress and dress mess uniforms. As I look back on that time, I believe it was the happiest day of Kimberly's life.

Of more than thirty-four hundred second lieutenants the army commissioned in 1998, fewer than two hundred were selected for aviation and only thirty-one of those were women.

Kimberly stayed at Presbyterian College until October, starting her army career as a Gold Bar recruiter. She recruited high school students from across Upstate South Carolina to college ROTC programs and set up an ROTC recruiting Web page. When she left for flight school, Lieutenant Colonel Mulhall recommended her for an Army Commendation medal, a rare accomplishment for a brand-new second lieutenant. Kimberly packed her bags and put Tiger, a gray tabby cat she'd adopted after graduation, in the car and drove to Ft. Rucker. It was time to fly.

CHAPTER 4

TIME TO FLY: 1998–2000

If I could ask Santa for anything in the world, it would be the ability to fly. I have always wanted to fly over the treetops like a bird, then swoop down to catch a newborn robin that fell out of its nest. If I could fly I would go to the Grand Canyon, then Paris and China. . . . If I could fly I would visit many places I will never get to go or see on land. Being able to fly is a lot to ask for, but someday it might happen.
—Kimberly Hampton, fourth grade Christmas book

A few weeks after finishing West Point, Travis McIntosh and Andy Reiter moved into a house at Ft. Rucker, Alabama, preparing to start flight school in October. They joined a local gym and spent a lot of time working out because their classes hadn't started yet. One night when Travis was at the gym without Andy, he struck up a conversation with an attractive young woman while he waited to use the machine she was on:

Immediately I could tell she was someone that I would like to know better. We discussed why we were both at Ft. Rucker. We were starting flight school and would be in the same class, we discovered. Of course that would be a good reason to exchange phone numbers.

They exchanged phone numbers and walked out of the gym together.

Lieutenant Colonel Larry Mulhall commissions Kimberly as a second lieutenant.

Travis was going to Atlanta to visit friends for a few days and said he'd call her when he got back.

When Travis returned, he unfolded the piece of paper from the gym. He looked at the name written neatly above the phone number. Kimberly Hampton. He dialed the number and asked her to go to dinner with him. They went to a restaurant near the base, ate wings, drank beer, and talked almost nonstop through the evening. The talked about their college experiences and they talked about flight school ahead. But Kimberly didn't tell Travis that she had started West Point with him. "She held that back. I didn't find that out until much later. As far as I knew she had spent all four years at Presbyterian College."

By the time flight school started, Kimberly and Travis were a couple. They worked out together, ran together, and studied together. Kimberly's fiercely competitive nature added a synergy to the relationship that pushed them both to excel and propelled them beyond what either one of them would have done alone.

Just getting into flight school is an accomplishment. It's a heavily competitive process, and it's even tougher for ROTC graduates than military academy graduates because there are fewer slots for them. Superior academic, military, and physical performance is needed through all four years of college to be considered for flight school.

Flight school takes most of a year, and not everyone makes it through the rigorous program. Kimberly, Travis and Andy were issued purple baseball caps that identified their class of about thirty young officers learning to fly helicopters. Each class had a different color ball cap. They called their purple hats "Barney" caps after the popular purple children's character.

The first month was spent in the classroom learning the systems that make up the helicopter, studying the fundamentals of aerodynamics and developing an understanding of weather patterns and wind turbulence. Then they began to split their days between the classroom and the flight line of small orange and white TH-67 Bell JetRanger helicopters that carry two students and one instructor. Slipping behind one of the three sets of controls, one for each hand and one for the feet, was a thrill for Kimberly. After the students learned how to operate the controls and how to start the helicopters they were ready for their "nickel ride," when they lift off the ground for the first time.

Following tradition, Kimberly handed the instructor a nickel with 1976, her birth year, on it – as she boarded the aircraft for her first flight. The instructor took the helicopter up for about half an hour and did the actual flying, but the students were allowed to put their hands on the controls while they flew.

After the nickel ride, students learn to hover and move between points just above the ground before going to a higher altitude. Kimberly was a natural. She was smooth and steady and had a knack for flying.

Kimberly was one of the first people to learn how to hover, which is a milestone for helicopter pilots. It can take several weeks to be able to smoothly control the aircraft at a hover.

After learning to hover, the students puddle-jumped across the southern Alabama countryside, alternately practicing take offs and landings as they flew between a series of fields that are designed like mini airports with landing strips about twenty-five to thirty miles apart. The student pilots honed their skills and eagerly waited for the instructor to grant them permission to fly solo. The solo flight is the next milestone, and permission isn't granted until the instructor feels the student is ready.

Kimberly and Travis made their solo flights on the same day, although not in the same aircraft. At the conclusion of their flights, they got their solo wings patches to wear on the front of their hats to show they've completed this critical step on the path to becoming a military aviator.

TRAVIS McINTOSH—

You get in a TH-67 helicopter, which is a little Bell JetRanger helicopter, and you and another flight student share the cockpit and you fly for the first time without an instructor on board at a small heliport. You can't really leave the airspace of the heliport, but you don't really want to at that point in your flying experience.

There was no real ceremony involved in sewing their solo wings onto their hats. Travis and Kimberly took the wings patches to a shop just outside the gate of the installation and got them sewn onto their purple Barney caps and took pictures of each other.

TRAVIS McINTOSH—

The best part is it set you apart from other flight students on Ft. Rucker. It lets people know where you are in your course of instruction; those with their solo wings on their hat compared to those who don't have it. You stand a little taller, shoulders a little further back and more confident.

The class had whittled down from about thirty students to twenty or twenty-five by the time everyone earned their solo wings, and they celebrated with a class party. Travis and Andy and their other housemates hosted the party because they had a pool. They chose a white-trash theme and scoured the local thrift shops for their costumes. If the wings on their caps were a point of pride, their white-trash outfits probably were not, but they videotaped the party and took pictures, for the record.

Kimberly found her calling during the next phase of flight school. The students moved from the TH-67s to the OH-58C, a basic version of the Kiowa helicopter she'd later fly in Iraq. It was back to the books to learn about oil pressures, temperatures and other mechanical knowledge that differs between different aircraft. Then it was time to start to learn basic combat skills and practice maneuvers needed for flying in potential conflict situations.

TRAVIS McINTOSH—

Flight school has its ups and downs. There are times when you feel like you're coasting through nice and easy and there are times when you're not sure how you're going to do. She enjoyed the tactics phase and the observation scout helicopters, which I believe ultimately led to her decision to select the OH-58 as her advanced aircraft. You learn to fly low and study the communications, the tactical radios, and you no longer feel like you are in the FAA's 'I'm gonna learn to be a pilot program.' It's the first exposure we had to becoming army aviators instead of just learning to fly. You could tell it had a significant impact on her because she enjoyed it much more.

Kimberly learned how to navigate flying low over treetops, how to find reference points from the air, and how to use a compass and to correct for winds. She learned how to read different shapes and colors that help pilots find things on the ground from the air and how to fly with night vision goggles when there's little light. The goggles make everything look sort of green and black and there's no depth perception. Kimberly learned how to compensate, because it's all too easy to fly up on something very quickly thinking it's farther away.

The final six weeks of flight school were less exciting and more of an officer training course to help the new second lieutenants understand their role as aviation leaders. It also was time for Kimberly and Travis to make career and personal decisions that would shape their futures.

They already had talked about the possibility of marriage and they wanted to stay together. To a large extent, their choice of aircraft would impact the likelihood of being stationed in the same place. Kimberly wanted to fly Kiowas. On her order of request she listed the OH-58 Delta (OH-58D) first, and then the Apache, Blackhawk, and Chinook, in that order, and got her first choice.

Travis chose the Blackhawk, a widely used transport aircraft because that would make it easier to follow Kimberly. The Kiowas were used in South Korea and that's where Kimberly wanted to go. With the exception of peacekeeping in Bosnia and Kosovo, Korea was the closest thing to a real world mission for the army at that time. It was where the action was and that's where Kimberly wanted to be.

Kimberly, Travis and Andy graduated from flight school on a blue and shiny day in August of 1999. They wore green Class A dress suit uniforms with all the awards and badges they'd acquired so far displayed on their coats. Their shoes were polished to a high gloss. Senior officers stood on the stage in front of a blue curtain and made the proper speeches to send the newly minted aviators out into the world.

Travis finished first in the class and Kimberly finished second. They had toggled back and forth between first and second all through flight school and when it came down to the wire, they knew it was close and they were both in the running to be first.

TRAVIS McINTOSH—

We could do the math. We knew it was coming down to either one of us toward the end. Both of us just took a mature approach to it. There is no number one. It didn't matter who got it. She is very competitive. It pushed us both to excel while we were there. It pushed both of us to exceed what we thought we could do.

The graduates were called onto the stage to receive certificates showing they had completed flight school and the date . . . and most importantly the silver flight wings aviators wear on their uniforms throughout their careers to show they made it.

Kimberly gives an impromptu speech during her commissioning ceremony at Presbyterian College. *Courtesy of Kenneth Lesley*

Dale and I watched the graduation ceremony proudly. Kimberly and Travis sat in the first two seats of the front row, which was reserved for the top graduates. Kimberly gave me a gold helicopter charm. I wore it on a necklace, just above my breastbone, close to my heart. I was so proud of my baby girl, all grown up.

Kimberly had an entourage there. My sister Frances and her husband Richard were there, and so was Donna Arnold. Kimberly was thrilled that her tennis coach had taken the time to be there, cheering her on as always.

They had a special ceremony when aviator wings were pinned on the top graduates. Travis went first and then Kimberly; the third and fourth top graduates in the class were next. They walked to the front of the room in the U.S. Army Aviation Museum where the ceremony was held. Each graduate was allowed to have one person come forward to pin on their new wings.

When Kimberly had been commissioned in a ceremony just prior to college graduation, Dale and I both had come forward and each of us pinned her second lieutenant bars to either shoulder.

This time there was only one set of wings, so only Dale went forward. I knew that for Kimberly this day ranked right up there with her commissioning. I was happy to see her so happy. The tears in my eyes were of pride and joy.

Kimberly outside the U.S. Army Aviation Museum at Ft. Rucker, Alabama, on her Flight School graduation day.

Proud father Dale pins on Kimberly's wings at Flight School graduation at Ft. Rucker, Alabama.

All of the graduates gave their family and friends a miniature set of wings. Dale put his actual set away for safekeeping and bought another set that he always wears on the left lapel of his jacket. He has worn those wings every time he's worn a suit jacket since that day, and I have worn my helicopter necklace every single day since then as well.

The new graduates received their assignments. Kimberly would finish her OH-58 qualification at Ft. Rucker, spend Christmas at home with us and then go to Camp Stanton, a small installation in northern South Korea near the DMZ in January. Travis would leave for Korea in November, two months ahead of Kimberly, and be based at Camp Stanley, a larger installation about forty miles southeast of Camp Stanton.

About a month before Travis left for Korea, Dale and I went with Kimberly and stayed with Travis and his parents for a few days. Travis and Dale were out on a run together when Travis asked him for Kimberly's hand in marriage.

CHAPTER 5

PILOT IN COMMAND: 2000–2001

---

amp Stanton, on the northwest side of South Korea, was nestled in a hilly rural area near Gwangtan, a village about fifteen kilometers from the DMZ, the demilitarized zone separating South and North Korea. It was an hour by car and fifteen minutes by air to the South China Sea. The camp was bisected by a noisy road, where "one-eyed buffalos," small diesel tractors with single headlights that pulled heavy-laden wagons, dodged big dump trucks dubbed "terminator trucks" because they rumbled back and forth to a nearby quarry and ran over anything in their way. The troops avoided the terminator trucks, too, and crossed the road on an overhead bridge that linked the two sides of the camp.

It was a small camp of about 180 people. There were two air troops, Delta and Echo. Foxtrot, or "Witchdoctor" Troop, as it was called by soldiers at Camp Stanton, was an aviation maintenance troop. Kimberly arrived in January of 2000, as the XO, or executive officer, for Foxtrot, the maintenance troop, and later became a platoon leader in Echo troop, historically called the "Horsemen" troop in the 4th Squadron of the 7th U.S. Calvary, General Custer's regiment.

Specialist Dave Gambrell, a maintenance crew chief in Foxtrot troop, noticed Kimberly sitting alone eating dinner her first night at Camp Stanton, on the other side of the globe from family and friends in Easley.

"She was new and didn't seem to know anyone, so I sat down beside her and asked where she was from."

He couldn't believe she was from Easley. Most of his family was from nearby Greenville. Within minutes they were chatting like old friends about Easley, Greenville, and Rock Springs Baptist Church. Rock Springs was Kimberly's church in Easley, and his aunt, uncle, and grandparents went there, too. Kimberly's first friend in Korea shared her memories of home:

> She was my XO and we became good friends. She had such a pleasant smile. She had a happy heart. I never heard her yell or scream or holler. In the military that's hard to believe. She would just say something, and the way she said it—silent thunder, I guess you would say. When something heavy happened, she was like the calm after the storm. She would take control in a subtle way. The way she would talk to you would let you know she had the confidence in you to do what needed to be done.
>
> She was more the administrative realm of the company. She would still fly, but as far as the maintenance activity, I didn't have that much interactivity with her. But it was a close knit group there. We were like a family.
>
> Enlisted personnel in the United States can't interact with officers - it's fraternization, but it's different in Korea. We were such a small group. It's an aviation post, and most of the people were warrant officers and pilots. They respected the maintenance crew and trusted our maintenance for the safety of the flight. And we had respect for them.

Officers at Camp Stanton lived in standard concrete block military barracks segregated by rank. Kimberly, now a lieutenant, lived on the first floor of the officers' barracks, near the laundry room. It was a convenient location except for the noise and traffic from the laundry. Chief Warrant Officer 2 Sean Jones, the senior pilot instructor for the troop, had the room next door. He loved to sing, but not in front of people. To unwind after a long day, he would go back to his room, shut the door for privacy, and turn up his music and sing. He didn't realize that his voice carried through the block wall:

One day I was getting into it really good, just singing my heart out, when all of a sudden there's this bang on my door. I turned my music down and ran to the door and opened it. There was Kimberly and she has got this grin, just ear to ear, and was just dying laughing. She knew she'd just busted me so bad.

"You can hear me, can't you?" I said, as my face turned beet red.

"Oh yeah, you're coming through loud and clear."

"Oh my God, I'm so embarrassed."

"Don't be. You sing beautifully."

"Well, that's good, because I'm not going to stop singing," I told her.

I never stopped singing and she never stopped smiling. She was the little sister I always wished I'd had. Everything you would ever want out of a little sister, that's what she was.

She was without a doubt the most professional officer and one of the best new pilots I'd ever seen. She was just a hard studier and put forth a lot of effort in trying to run the job and really impressed me. It's a rarity to see somebody like that, somebody who goes above and beyond.

She was really having some rough times, trying to get a grasp on what it meant to be a lieutenant and a leader and a pilot. At that time, my wife was pregnant and living in Colorado. We were about to have our first kid, and there I was all the way in Korea. Both of us were trying to find somebody to confide in. She was the one person I could come to and just talk like family, real people stuff. One night we were out talking and I made her a deal that I would teach her everything I could about being an officer and a pilot if she'd just be that one person that I could come and talk non-army stuff to. Our friendship was pretty much born on that day and just grew from there.

The Horsemen flew reconnaissance for the 2nd Infantry Division. Chief Warrant Officer 3 John "Mac" MacElroy, an instructor pilot in Kimberly's circle of friends, described their aerial missions as "a speed bump" to discourage the North Koreans from coming south.

Winters were frigid and the summers were as hot and humid as New

Kimberly in her cavalry Stetson standing next to a Kiowa helicopter on the flight line in Korea.

Kimberly in her cavalry Stetson and leather jacket in a Camp Stanton, Korea, restaurant.
Courtesy of Sean Jones

York City. Days started early, with PT at 6:30 AM. Everybody had to be there unless they were flying afternoons or nights. The troops were always on alert, on duty or off.

"When the horn went off you had to rush out to your aircraft and be all cranked up and ready to go to receive a mission," Mac said.

Kimberly thrived on the adrenalin in the atmosphere. She was excited about being in the cavalry and in South Korea. It was where the action was, but there was some security in knowing that it was unlikely that anyone would shoot at you. It was the closest thing to a real world mission for the army at that time except for peacekeeping in Bosnia and Kosovo.

Kimberly and Travis tried to see each other on weekends but didn't get to spend nearly as much time together as they'd hoped. Travel was difficult. The forty miles between the two camps would have been an easy trip back home, but it was a long distance to travel in South Korea. The trip took hours on the army bus that stopped at every crossroads. It was faster to take a train, but train service was available only part of the way. The rest of the trip was by taxi, and between the language barrier and the cost, taxi rides weren't a good option either.

One day when Kimberly was flying, she spotted Travis from the air practicing maneuvers at an abandoned airstrip. She radioed him and they flew together for about fifteen minutes back toward their respective camps, until she had to turn west toward Camp Stanton while he continued south. It was a glorious day. Just a short time ago they were learning to hover in flight school in Alabama. Now they were here flying advanced aircraft on the other side of the world. It was a culmination of everything they'd worked for. Before they parted ways, Travis flew his Blackhawk to the left of Kimberly's Kiowa and took a picture, freezing the moment in time.

As soon as the opportunity arose, Kimberly made a trip south of Seoul to Osan, where there was an Air Force base. She was on a shopping mission. She wanted a brown leather flight jacket from a certain leather goods shop just outside the base. It was a hallmark for American cavalry officers.

Everybody got their brown leather aviator flight jackets at Osan, Mac said. It was the thing to do. Every Friday, everybody would wear Stetsons and flight jackets.

It was a warm day, and Mac was in the shop looking for a leather motorcycle jacket to wear when he got back to the States. He was wearing his usual off-duty uniform, a pair of hiking shorts and hiking boots. It was a "really horrible look," he said. He was trying on a jacket and a pair of seatless leather riding chaps when Kimberly walked in. She looked at his shorts sticking out of the rear of the chaps, his big hiking boots, and burst out laughing. Much to Mac's embarrassment, she pulled out her camera and snapped a picture that he knew would make the rounds of the camp.

"It was a Kodak moment. It was just horrible, absolutely horrible. She never went anywhere without that damn camera," Mac said.

Whenever Kimberly could find down time, she got away from camp to explore the country. The culture and traditions of Korea intrigued her. Everything was new and different and she wanted to learn about all of it. She and Travis took walks through the various markets filled with open air fruit stands, vegetable stands, and vendors who sold every little trinket imaginable. There were linens and rugs, fish and chicken. The farmers came out early in the morning. It was fascinating to watch them conduct business. Kimberly enjoyed the Korean food, and one of her greatest delights was to discover a clean and neat little restaurant tucked away like a peaceful oasis amid the busy commercial activity.

She had a chance to show off some of the interesting places she'd discovered when I came to visit in July. It was my first trip overseas. Putting my luggage through customs and the long flight were intimidating, and I was more than a little scared at the thought of going to a foreign country where people spoke a language I didn't understand. But I was going to see my baby girl. That was all that mattered.

A welcoming party was waiting for me when I arrived at the Seoul airport. Travis and another officer were there with Kimberly. She looked good. She looked happy. I got the feeling that it was a pretty big deal to have family visit a place so far away. We spent some time in Seoul, and I also stayed at Camp Stanton with Kimberly. While at Camp Stanton, I made the acquaintance of Mrs. Han, a precious Korean woman, who worked on the base and had kind of adopted Kimberly.

"Don't you worry. Hampton, she my daughter. I take care of her," she told me. I liked her right off the bat. I knew Mrs. Han really would look out after Kimberly.

It was fascinating to see where Kimberly was living and what she was doing but I was never completely at ease on our forays into the country-side. It was so different from anything I'd ever experienced and certainly lacked most of the comforts of home. Kimberly, on the other hand was so happy there. She really loved Korea. She enjoyed her work and she enjoyed the people she met.

One day she took me to Panmunjeom, where negotiations that ended the Korean War took place, and we visited the Joint Security Area on the North Korean border in the DMZ. It's the only place where North and South Korea connect, and military guards watch over each side. Security is tight. We were briefed beforehand, and warned not to wave or make any type of contact with the North Korean guards. Both countries have build-ings on their own sides, and there also are some United Nations buildings. In one United Nations buildings right on the demarcation line that sepa-rates the two countries, we went into a conference room, under guards' watchful eyes, where a meeting table is placed right on the line.

We also went through a tunnel to a closed door on the demarcation line. North Korea was on the other side of the door. We turned around at the door and went back the way we came. The whole thing was somber and sobering.

I can't say that the experience made me feel any better about where my baby girl was stationed. If anything, despite her excitement and enthusi-asm, it probably fueled my imagination for the worse. Still, I wouldn't take anything for the mother-daughter time, as unusual as it was. It was worth it all just to be with Kimberly.

That fall Kimberly went on her spur ride, a tradition and milestone for those in the cavalry. The spur ride itself is more than twenty-four hours of grueling physical and mental challenges for soldiers on their first cavalry assignment. Kimberly was part of a group of about thirty who earned their spurs together. They took off at 5:00 AM, and hiked through the hilly Korean countryside with a map and compass to various stations where they had to perform different tasks. Sean oversaw a simulated ambush operation at one of the stations. Kimberly and the others were instructed to go to a certain grid on a map and perform a reconnaissance action. Unbeknownst to them, fake enemy personnel were lying in ambush, and they had to fend off a mock attack. Each station held a different challenge. It was nearly lunch time the next day when the weary soldiers finally got to rest and soak their aching feet before a ceremony when they received their well-earned spurs.

Dave Gambrell married a Korean woman, and Kimberly found a new friend and a local restaurant guide. Dave's new wife knew all the best restaurants, and Kimberly loved to meet them at different restaurants for dinner. Sometimes they'd invite her to dinner at their home in the village outside the camp, and they'd all talk for hours over the meal.

When the Gambrells' first child was born, Kimberly surprised them at the hospital room with a big bouquet of flowers. The baby was only three or four hours old, and Dave asked her if she wanted to hold the baby. He recalled how comfortable she appeared as she smiled down at the tiny girl:

> She was the only person in that whole installation that came. My wife and I will never forget that day. Kimberly was the third person in this world that held my beautiful daughter. The first time I held the baby, I was kind of shaking. I was scared I was going to drop her. She knew how to hold a baby. I could see it in her eyes that she was looking forward to the day that she would have a child and hold it in her arms.

Several times a year Camp Stanton hosted children from a local orphanage, and Kimberly always looked forward to their visits. An American style dinner was waiting when the children came to the camp on Thanksgiving. They didn't quite understand what the American holiday was all about, but they enjoyed the attention and the break from their usual routine. When the children returned at Christmas, everyone sang carols after dinner and then Santa came and surprised them with gifts. Kimberly, like most of the soldiers, sponsored one or two children and bought gifts for them. It was hard to tell whether the soldiers or the children enjoyed the exchanges more.

Interacting with the children helped soldiers who had children at home cope with being away from their families. Kimberly just loved the chance to share a smile and watch the children laugh and have fun. One day Kimberly volunteered to help take some of the orphans to an amusement park in Seoul. The outing was an adventure on the scale of a trip to Disneyland for these Korean children.

A Korean colonel at a nearby base heard that Kimberly played tennis

Kimberly at a gunnery exercise in a remote field in Korea.

Kimberly and a furry friend at Korean Village on Christmas Eve 2000, during a visit from Mom and Dad.

and she gained a tennis partner as well as an adoptive family. After their
tennis games, she often went to the colonel's home for dinner. She tutored
his children in English and played tennis with them. When Kimberly was
promoted to the rank of captain before she left Korea, the colonel and
his wife attended the ceremony. He gave her a bouquet of long stemmed
yellow roses befitting a beauty queen and presented her with a Korean
captain's hat. It looked like a giant Elmer Fudd hat and clashed with her
uniform, but that didn't bother Kimberly a bit. She put the hat on immediately and cherished the gift.

Every Thursday night Kimberly volunteered to teach English to the
Korean soldiers stationed at the camp. The group of about ten Koreans
already spoke some English and served as camp translators. The English
instruction was mandatory for the Korean translators, but because they
already were somewhat fluent, Kimberly didn't want them to be bored, so
she turned the lessons into freewheeling group discussions around a big
table in a conference room they used as a classroom. Under her tutelage
their speaking skills and vocabularies grew along with cultural understanding and friendship.

While Kimberly was making friends in Korea, time and distance started
to erode her relationship with Travis. It was difficult to take time off to
visit each other, and while Kimberly focused on her career, she and Travis
drifted apart. They met one morning at an installation about halfway
between the two camps to shop for groceries and broke off their engagement over an emotional lunch.

Meanwhile, Kimberly's career was taking off. She was becoming a
better and better pilot. Sean decided she was ready for the next step:

The biggest thing for a new pilot is that first real hurdle of becoming a pilot-in-command. You are in charge of your own aircraft at
that point. It's like being sixteen and being handed the keys to the
car. It's just an overwhelming responsibility.

I approached her while we were in gunnery, where we go out
and live in a field for thirty days and shoot bullets and rockets off
of our aircraft.

"How confident do you feel about becoming a pilot-in-command?"

"Sean, there's so much I have to learn. I don't think I'm ready."

"That's probably the first sign that you are ready, when you realize you still have a lot to learn. I think you're ready, and I talked to the commander and he thinks you're ready too."

We agreed to give her a pilot-in-command ride, which is a fairly lengthy check ride that consists of a lengthy formal evaluation where I ask her non-stop aviation questions. Then we go out and she has to perform two different flights. One is all mission and tactical oriented, and the second one is what we call an instrument evaluation, where she flies approaches just using the aircraft's instrument systems. She breezed through the oral evaluation like I knew she would, and she breezed through the tactical flight itself, like I knew she would.

The next day we set up the second flight, to go down to a place called Camp Humphreys, which was a fairly large camp in Korea. We were north of Stanton in a field site, so the flight was probably about an hour and a half. Of course she breezed through the entire instrument portion and we landed at Camp Humphreys.

"While we're here we might as well get something to eat," I told her.

Since we'd been in a field for two or three weeks at that time eating MREs and living on cots, she thought it was quite a good idea too. You weren't going to pass up real food.

We went to this place, an Italian restaurant at Camp Humphreys. The name of the place is Sarducchi's. That was the second time I'd been stationed in Korea. The first time I was stationed at Camp Humphreys. As we walked up to the restaurant I was telling her about some of the worst exploits I'd had the first time I was there, ten years earlier, to get her kind of eased up, because she didn't know whether or not she had passed. When we went in the restaurant I told her, 'Look, it was an excellent evaluation and you're going to be a pilot-in-command.' I told her I really appreciated what a great job she did. A lot of people put a lot of effort into a pilot-in-command check ride, but she went well above and beyond. It was unbelievably impressive and made my life easy as an evaluator.

For celebration, we got these wine glasses. They were sitting on the table, but we had to fly back, so it was not like she could have a glass of wine or anything, so we wound up getting tea in these wine glasses. We sipped it and ate our dinner and we just had a good time.

"You're gonna look back on today and you're gonna remember this day forever."

"We need something to commemorate this day."

I hate to say it, but I liberated those two wine glasses from the restaurant. It was not very officer-like of me. When we got away from the restaurant I handed her one and she giggled.

"Sean, what are you doing?"

"You're gonna remember this every time you look at this wine glass sitting on your shelf."

We wound up getting weathered in at Camp Humphreys and couldn't make it back until the next day. The weather became really bad. It was raining with very low clouds and fog. It was pretty bad. We had to go all the way up north by the DMZ to the field site, and had to go through this little mountain pass. All that was completely fogged in, so we wound up staying the night at one of the villages outside of Camp Humphreys in a Korean motel.

The next day we flew back IFR: that's instrument flight rules in real aviation terms, but as a joke pilots call it "I follow roads," which means the weather is so bad that all you see is a road and you follow a road and it takes you where you want to go.

We ended up getting back and everybody congratulated her on her pilot-in-command. We were at the end of our field problem so for her first flight as a pilot-in-command I gave her one of the most junior pilots so that she knew for a fact that she was in charge of this aircraft. She wasn't going to get some old crusty aviator and just be the so called pilot-in-command. She knew she was actually in charge. She flew all the way home, her first real flight as a pilot-in-command, with this junior pilot next to her. He was taking pictures with his little digital camera, so it goes to show you how much help he was.

I told him when they landed to distract her so we could come around and do a little pilot-in-command ceremony. So she landed and shut down the aircraft and at that point he's telling her that he wants to take pictures of her, with her first pilot-in-command flight being over. What she doesn't realize is up on the other side of her, I'm standing just outside the door waiting for her to open the door. So as she steps out of the aircraft I grab her and then all the pilots in the troop come running over with this big bucket of cold water—this gray plastic five-gallon can of cold water, and just drenched her completely from head to toe. It was a chilly day to begin with. She was just soaked to the bone. There was one huge smile on that woman's face. It was an incredible time.

One summer Sunday afternoon in 2000, Kimberly was headed out on a ten-mile run when the commanding officer, Bill Gerrard, stopped her and introduced her to a young captain named Will Braman who was visiting the camp and looking at some of the equipment. The commander told Kimberly that Captain Braman was coming in as the new commander. Kimberly didn't know that Captain Gerrard was leaving and was a bit miffed that he hadn't told her sooner.

"It's news to me," she retorted in a tone of voice that made it obvious to the incoming commander that if she wasn't in charge officially, she definitely had clout. He was also a bit concerned that he was going to have to keep up with a lieutenant who could run ten miles on a whim.

After Captain Braman officially took command, he and Kimberly worked together on a daily basis. As the senior platoon leader, she was his next-in-command. Their strengths and weaknesses complemented each other, and before long they could anticipate each other's moves. He never had to worry about whether she was going to do the right thing. She just stepped up and got things done and always seemed to anticipate what he needed to keep the unit running strong.

I went back to Korea at Christmas. This was supposed to be Dale's trip because I went in July, but I wanted to go again so badly and my boss let me take the time. It didn't start off well. We got to the Greenville airport and found out our flight had been cancelled. We got on another flight and nearly missed our connection in Japan. We had to run through the airport but we made it. It was all worthwhile when we came down the escalator in Seoul and saw Kimberly.

Kimberly smiles for photograph after landing at Camp Stanton, Korea,
at the end of her first flight as a pilot-in-command.

We had a room at the Dragon Hill Lodge at Yongsan Garrison, a U.S. Army base in Seoul. It was modern, comfortable, and extremely nice, and much like any nice hotel you'd find here at home. The weather was terrible. Christmas Eve day was bitterly cold. Kimberly took us to the Korean Folk Village. We took a train part of the way and a bus the rest of the way. It took more than an hour to get there. Korean folk dancers put on an acrobatic show and there were houses that were representative of the Korean culture. We were outside and it was freezing, but we all particularly enjoyed the dancers and their acrobatic talents. On the way out Kimberly had to have her picture taken hugging a furry donkey at one of the housing exhibits. We found a little gift shop and it was warm inside and we stayed a little too long. We missed the last bus out. It was already dark and the temperature was dropping. Kimberly said she'd call a taxi. The taxi took us to the closest bus stop. People were packed in the bus. Every time it stopped and people got off even more people got on. The ride took forever. The bus must have stopped every two hundred feet. Kimberly and I finally got seats but Dale never did. The bus took us back to the train. Once we got on the train everything was okay again. We weren't packed in there. We all got to sit down, and we knew where we were going. But we had learned that travel in Korea could be difficult.

Kimberly spent the night with us at the hotel instead of going back to

Kimberly is showered with cold water at Camp Stanton in Korea following her first flight as a pilot-in-command.

Camp Stanton. Dale went to bed and Kimberly and I stayed up late talking. Shortly before midnight Kimberly said, "Look out the window."

It was snowing. It was coming down in big soft flakes. It was Christmas and it was beautiful.

"Guess what happened overnight," Dale said when we woke up on Christmas morning.

"It snowed," we said, completely taking the wind out of his sails.

The roads were icy under the new fallen snow. Our plan for the day was to go up to Camp Stanton. We called several taxis before we found one that was willing to take us there with the snow and ice. The trip would take about an hour under optimal conditions. We rode for about two-and-a-half hours. The roads were slick with ice and they were narrow and full of twists and turns. This would be Dale's first look at Camp Stanton and I hoped he'd get to see it. I wondered if we would make it there.

We finally arrived. The guys had cooked Christmas dinner on hot plates, ham and all the trimmings. It was absolutely wonderful. Their ability to cook a meal like this on hot plates was unbelievable. We brought Christmas gifts and participated in a gift exchange. I got some Korean wind chimes that I hung on the screened porch of the lake house when I got home. The day passed quickly and it was time to go, but once again we had transportation problems. The roads were still icy and we couldn't get a taxi to go up there. I wanted to just stay the night at Camp Stanton, but Kimberly said she'd get us back. She and another officer walked with us to Gwang-tan, the closest town, although that's using the term "town" loosely. There was a cluster of shacks there and that's about all. There was a restaurant, and it was like an old shack with long tables, but Kimberly and some of the others from the base often would walk down for inexpensive all-you-can-eat dinners there. The road was covered with snow and ice. I hung on to Dale's arm for dear life. The walk took about 15 minutes. We got a taxi there and because of the language barrier, Kimberly and the other officer came along. The taxi carried us a short distance to a bus and then we took the bus to the train station and got back to Seoul. We spent a few more days sightseeing and Dale flew back home to get to work, but I stayed for New Year's Eve.

The Dragon Hill Lodge was the place to be. There was music and food, the place was packed, and I saw the New Year in with my baby girl.

July 5, 2001
I have been serving as an aeroscout platoon leader for about 10 months and I hope to

Kimberly is promoted
to the rank of captain
at Camp Stanton, Korea.

keep this job until I leave. Most lieutenants get about six months of platoon leader time in Korea, so I'm lucky to have kept this job as long as I have. It has been a wonderful experience so far. I have 4-6 warrant officers and 5-7 enlisted crew chiefs in my platoon at any one time. I have been blessed with great soldiers, which has made my job easy. I get to fly quite a bit—it's awesome. Korea is a beautiful place (from the air at least) with hills, mountains and more rice paddies than you can imagine.

I wouldn't trade my time here for anything. We are reminded in many ways each day that we are doing a great thing not only for our country but also for the South Korean people. For the most part they are grateful for our presence and our commitment to deter North Korean aggression.

—Kimberly's e-mail to a group of friends and family

On September 11, 2001, as terrorist hijackers boarded planes in New York City and began to carry out a plot that soon would send tens of thousands of troops to Afghanistan and Iraq, the air troops at Camp Stanton were planning and rehearsing for a large night air assault training event. It was a fairly elaborate mission and the mood was intense. Suddenly a staff duty officer who had a TV on began to shout about an aircraft flying into the World Trade Center. The day is etched in Mac's memory:

Everything stopped. We gathered around the TV and saw the second aircraft hit. It was pretty surreal.

After we realized there was nothing we were going to be called on to do that night, we went back to our planning and our rehearsals. We were just going to control the things we could control. Our job was to keep driving on with our missions to show the North Koreans how rock steady we were, by doing what it is that we needed to do, and other forces would take care of their responsibilities. We had a specific mission, and we needed to continue to do it.

We went out to where the air assault was, for the rehearsal and the walk through. There was a large aviation task force out in the field that we were going to go out and support. The brigade commander called a formation in the field and explained to everybody who had been isolated and hadn't heard the news what had happened.

Dale called me at the office that morning and I knew when I heard his voice something was up. He wouldn't call me at work for causal conversation. He told me there had been a huge accident and a plane had hit the World Trade Center, and before I could get up and go check the Internet he called back and told me that a second plane had hit and it obviously was an act of terrorism.

Word started spreading, and in a large office environment it doesn't take long for people to start getting upset. We had a portable television in one of the offices and we left it on all day and kept going by and checking to see what was happening.

Rumors were flying and people kept coming by and asking me, "Have you heard from Kimberly?"

I was concerned for her, and at that point I didn't know anything about the Taliban. I was worried that this could be a Communist plot to overthrow, and there she was just a few miles from North Korea and I feared they could be coming down and attacking.

I tried not to think about it and focus on my work instead, but it was almost impossible. All day long people kept coming by my desk and asking about Kimberly and each time my fears increased.

When I had visited Kimberly in Korea, it was interesting to see what she was doing and the places she went to, but it also made me worry more. On that first visit, she had taken me through a neighborhood up into the hilly terrain outside of Camp Stanton, where she ran every day. It was in a scary place for me, partly because of the unknown, and partly because living conditions were so different from what I was accustomed to. Kimberly thought it was a fantastic place. When she ran, people would recognize her and would wave or speak as she went by. Of course we walked the day I went with her, we didn't run.

I remembered how nervous I felt and the tension in the atmosphere the day we visited Panmunjeom, on the North Korean border in the DMZ.

I thought about Mrs. Han, and how she had reassured me that she was watching out for Kimberly. I wondered what Kimberly and Mrs. Han were doing and whether they were in any danger.

It was a great relief to hear Kimberly's voice on the phone when she called early that afternoon. She made separate calls to Dale and me at our offices.

Just answering the phone and hearing her voice say, "Hey, Mommie," —it always was music to my ears, and it particularly was that day.

It was obvious she had been as worried about us as we were about her.

"What are you doing at work. You're in a high rise building. Go home," she told me.

I assured her that we were okay and told her I couldn't just leave, but she was extremely worried about me.

It was all so surreal. She was in Korea and worried about us here at home, where we had always felt so safe. It really didn't sink in at the time that this could mean she'd eventually go into real combat.

At that point, I felt her time in Korea, flying close to the DMZ, was the most dangerous situation she would ever be in. Every day that she was in Korea I worried about her proximity to the DMZ, the dangers of flying along the border and the possibility of wire strikes while she was flying.

On September 11, I was still in that mode of thinking that bad things happen somewhere else, they don't happen this close to home.

It took a long time before the full impact of that tragic day dawned on me in terms of my child's life. It wasn't until she went to Iraq two years later that it really hit me.

The terrorist attacks changed life for Americans everywhere. Security tightened and Camp Stanton was no exception. Kimberly told me they were on the highest alert status. Personnel were fairly restricted in their movements and there were few recreational forays away from the camp. Kimberly's days of freely roaming the countryside were over.

Everyone was cooped up on the small base together. The officers wanted a place where they could let their hair down, away from the enlisted soldiers, so they got together and transformed a dayroom into a bar they called the Babushka Lounge. The name came from an insult shouted by some Russian mafia types trying to drum up business for the local dives away from the camp. "Babushkas!" the Russians taunted Americans who passed them by without going in. It was the Russian word for grandmother.

The officers built a tiki hut over the top of the bar and hung camouflage netting entwined with Christmas lights from the ceiling. They found some bar stools, a pool table, dart boards, and a big screen TV. The Babushka Lounge had all the comforts of home.

WILL BRAMAN—

It just turned out to be a great social center for all the officers and senior enlisted guys there. It was pretty amazing. It all was built with about fifteen core people finding barstools here and tearing apart old wall lockers to make the bar top and some very skilled craftsmen we didn't know we have making the best they could out of pretty austere conditions. It was a great place to go to after flying and on the weekends, and that's pretty much what we did. It was a sight to be seen. It went from a room with some couches and a pool table to a full bar with a pool table and big screen TV, dart boards and camouflage netting hanging from the ceiling with Christmas lights, and murals on the wall. It was pretty impressive by the time we left.

While activities at the Babushka—and procurement of some of the items in there—resembled episodes of the old *M*A*S*H* television series, the events of 9-11 cast a more serious shadow across the minds of soldiers serving far from home.

There was laughter in the Babushka Lounge, but the officers began to realize that the next few years would be very different for them. One October day, Kimberly and Captain Braman went hiking in the mountains near the camp, and talked about how the events of September 11 would impact their careers:

She was talking about her future and where she wanted to go next and where she wanted to command a troop. I remember specifically saying, "Your time as troop commander and leading troops is going to be very different from mine. The future is very uncertain right now. You are going to go to combat somewhere and lead troops into combat. By the time you get to where you're going, we're going to be in the middle of whatever plays out from the result of this thing."

We had a long talk about that and the responsibilities that she was going to have. They are always there as a commander, but as a commander in combat, it's going to be even more difficult and even more important of a job that she was going to have to do. I think she realized that. The possibility of something going on in Korea, there was always a chance, but it was in back of your mind. You

Kimberly with Korean children on an outing to an amusement park in Seoul.

were mostly doing training, preparing for things. I think she realized her training time was over, and when she got to her next unit she was going to be acting on everything she'd learned up to that point. She took that very seriously.

I definitely saw a change in her when she left, knowing that her next step was going to be someplace where she was going to be ultimately responsible for everybody. I saw it play out when she was over in Iraq. Her attitude toward her people, she was very possessive about making sure her people were okay and doing the right thing and not unnecessarily being put in harm's way, which ultimately resulted in her death.

She had the opportunity not to fly that mission, but as dangerous as she knew it was going to be, she couldn't ask somebody else to do it and sit back at home. She chose to lead.

Kimberly and her cat Tiger at her home at Ft. Rucker.

CHAPTER 6

THE CAPTAINS COURSE

H ome from Korea, Kimberly's next step up the army career ladder was the Captains Career Course, so it was back to "Mother Rucker," as the aviators called Ft. Rucker, to work on professional skills. Once again Kimberly found herself in the midst of a unique group of people whose personalities fit together as closely as pieces of a jigsaw puzzle. Unlike flight school, there was little homework and plenty of time for camaraderie. It probably was the most laid back, relaxed time of Kimberly's adult life.

It was not high pressure. In college, it was always tennis, studying, ROTC. She was always under the gun, staying up all night. As an English major, she had a lot of papers to do and books to read. In flight school she was motivated and driven to do well and there was a lot to learn. The Captains Course was different.

There were about seventy or so new army captains in the course at the time. They were broken up into smaller groups of about fifteen each. Everybody in Kimberly's small group meshed.

CAPTAIN LEO LESCH—

We all just became the best of friends. The guys were brothers and Kimberly was our sister. It was neat that way, because being in different units in the army, sometimes you just show up for work and you do your job and go home and you

*don't want to deal with the people around you. This was just so different. We
all gleaned from each other's experiences. We couldn't get enough of each other.*

*We planned trips together. We had a lot in common. Riding motorcycles.
About 10 of us had motorcycles. We bonded that way. After class we'd go out
and ride our motorcycles and hang out at each other's house, or just go for pizza.*

*Everyone had Harleys except one guy had a Honda, and we harassed him
for that. I had a Harley Ultra Classic. I got harassed. The other guys called
my bike a 'grandpa's bike' because they had the smaller bikes. We rode quite
a bit. It took a long time to get Kimberly on anyone's bike. She said if her
parents found out about it they would kill us. It was always a big secret.*

*In the classroom, Kimberly was the consummate professional in dealing with
individuals. She was very assertive, but she knew how to be assertive without
being forceful. At times you have to make a decision and go with it. Kimberly
had no issues with that. When Kimberly made a decision, you could bet she had
thought it through and was going to stick to it. Unless you could come up with
a really, really good reason for her to change her mind, it wasn't going to happen.*

*She got a lot of harassment from us as far as a sister and brother relation-
ship. She always took it with a big smile. She never took it personally. It was
just fun. It just goes back to being a leader and not assimilating to the group
think idea.*

*We were all A-plus-plus-plus personalities. That's when Afghanistan was
kicking off and where ever we had to go, we all wanted to get there, to catch up
with whatever was ahead of us.*

*Our group pretty much stuck together. We didn't have very many outsiders
come into our group or very many people leave our group and hang out with the
other groups.*

*You have PT in the mornings, at 6:00 AM. A big part of the Captains
Course physical training is Ultimate Frisbee. You play that two days of every
week and then there's a big tournament at the end. When we got on the Ultimate
Frisbee court, it was a lot of fun. Some teams just exploded on the court. We
just embraced each other and played to each other's strengths. That's what the
group always did. I think that kept us all together. Rather than focusing on
each other's weaknesses, we focused on each other's strengths and their experiences
and what they had to offer. We just melded into a fantastic group.*

*It's not time that creates bonds. It's events, personalities, and maybe crises.
We created a family from the get-go and I still don't know why or how it*

happened that way. Anyone from our time probably would say it was the best experience in their military career up to that point.

Kimberly's group bonded like a high school clique. They watched Busch races on Saturdays and NASCAR races on Sundays. They made several weekend motorcycle trips to Florida beaches in Panama City, Destin, and Ft. Walton. During Beach Week they went to a time share condo on the Panama City beach and partied like twenty-year-olds on spring break.

They teased and tormented each other like siblings, and they teased Kimberly unmercifully, but they also took care of her. The men liked to get together and cook. Kimberly was no Betty Crocker. She liked to nap on the sofa while they cooked.

"Kimberly doesn't have to cook. She has us," one of the men told Dale and me during one of our visits. After Korea, it was good to have Kimberly at a place we could drive to and call whenever we wanted. Kimberly and I talked on the phone almost every day. Kimberly always had stories to tell me about their pranks. After worrying so much about her flying near the DMZ in Korea, it was so nice to be able to talk and laugh together and know she was in a safe and happy place.

One time, she told me on the phone, she was taking a nap and all of a sudden she heard the guys giggling. She knew they were up to something. They had mousetraps that they were snapping right in front of her face to wake her up. They were always up to something. It was like she had lots of mischievous brothers.

Kimberly decided to enter an Iron Aviator competition that spring. The guys tried to talk her out of it. It would be a lot of work, and it would be more fun to sit on the sidelines and watch, they argued. This contest was right up Kimberly's alley and she stood firm.

Contestants had to ride a bicycle, run with a rucksack filled with rocks and swim. Kimberly started training about a month before the event. She rode her bicycle to class a couple days a week and worked on her swimming. Since she already was a serious runner and had a bicycle, swimming was her weakest area and she trained hard. She expected to do well in the first two legs of the competition and didn't want to lose when she hit the pool at the end.

The others in her group all rallied around her. Kimberly was the racecar and they were her pit crew. Everyone woke up early on the day of the race to help load Kimberly's bicycle and rucksack. They lined up their lawn chairs to watch and cheer her on. When Kimberly came into the changing area after the first leg of the race, her pit crew was waiting. They changed her shoes like NASCAR crews change tires on a car. One pulled off her left shoe and another pulled off the right one, new shoes went on and she was off again. When she returned to the changing area to change for the swimming event, she had the lead in the women's division, but they could tell she was hurting. The long race was brutal.

Her pit crew went into action. One lifted her by the armpits. Others pulled off the clothing she wore over her bathing suit. She raced for the pool and dove in. Another woman was catching up fast. The men screamed at the tops of their voices to urge Kimberly on.

If Kimberly could keep up the pace, she had it in the bag, but swimming was her weakest event. Kimberly was a lap ahead when the next woman hit the pool moments later. It was nip and tuck. The woman nearly caught up when Kimberly pulled ahead again. The men were hoarse from cheering. The distance between the two women narrowed and widened, but Kimberly never gave up the lead. It was within a lap at times, but Kimberly was a lap and a half ahead when she touched the edge of the pool at the finish, smiling from ear to ear. The guys ran up and grabbed her up in a group hug.

Kimberly won the women's division, and they shared in her victory.

May 22 was graduation day. The ceremony was at the aviation museum. Kimberly was an honor graduate near the top of her class, and her group had come in second in the Ultimate Frisbee competition. Dale and I watched the ceremony with pride in Kimberly's accomplishment, and kept our thoughts to ourselves afterward as Kimberly and her group gathered all the motorcycles in front of the museum for one last picture together at Ft. Rucker.

"You aren't riding those motorcycles are you," Dale had asked her one time. She just shrugged. She never denied it, but she never admitted it. But Dale and I knew. The dead give away was a burn on her leg. She had hopped on a motorcycle with shorts on. It was so bad that she had to be taken to the infirmary. She couldn't hide it any more.

The day was bittersweet, but it wasn't quite time for goodbyes yet. The entire class traveled to Ft. Leavenworth, Kansas, for six weeks of training necessary for them to function as staff officers, including computer software instruction. The course was an easy task for the aviators, who had done a lot of this type of work in the Advanced Course.

Some of the guys rode their bikes to Ft. Leavenworth. One pulled a trailer with a bunch of others. Kimberly drove in her car. They timed their arrival so they could move into the same hallway. It was like living in a college dorm and the aviators made the most of their final weeks together, their last fling before going their separate ways and rejoining the real world as army leaders in a new War on Terrorism. They rode the bikes to Kansas City on the weekends, played golf, and kept creating memories.

They left Ft. Leavenworth on July 3. It was my birthday. Kimberly told me she was going to visit some friends after she left Ft. Leavenworth, but she drove straight to our lake house and arrived the next day. It was a birthday surprise for me, and Dale was in on the plan.

My back was to the door when Kimberly arrived with flowers and a cake.

"Wouldn't it be nice if Kimberly could be here?" Dale casually asked me when he saw Kimberly walking to the door.

I was responding as Kimberly made her entrance and I screamed and grabbed her in a hug. The memory of that day is priceless!

Kimberly reported to Ft. Bragg in early August and rented a house in Fayetteville. It was a good sized suburban ranch style home in a nice neighborhood about a mile from Leo who also went to Ft. Bragg after the Captains Course. It had a large fenced yard and was more than what a typical single person might need, but Kimberly expected to be at Ft. Bragg for at least three years and hoped to get a command. If she did, she wanted a place big enough for troop get-togethers. She liked the big yard, too, because she eventually wanted to get a dog.

Kimberly worked in the S3 operations shop for the 82nd Aviation Brigade at Ft. Bragg, a coveted job for any upwardly mobile young officer because it offers the opportunity to work for a major and get to know the company commanders.

"That's where all the movers and shakers hang out. It offers a lot of visibility and you are in charge of planning and execution of battalion missions," Leo said.

Kimberly worked for Capt. Manuel Hernandez, who managed the operations shop. "Chief," as everyone called him, had returned from Afghanistan about two months before Kimberly arrived at Ft. Bragg and was anxious to get an assistant. He was a senior captain and Kimberly was a new captain, so although he was her supervisor, they were peers. Chief hoped that wouldn't be a problem.

It wasn't. If Chief needed something, "Without hesitation she'd get it for me," he said. "She wasn't one to stand around and wait for work to be done. She would ask, 'What do you need? What else do we need to get done?' " Kimberly wasn't worried about rank; she was a team player and the goal was to get the job done and done well. Chief found it easy to be both her supervisor and a friend.

"Business was business, but as peers we'd go out to lunch often, several times a week, and spend that hour talking about stuff, our military careers and where we saw ourselves," Chief said. It was a great working environment for both of them, but it was a challenging time for Kimberly. Working with Chief helped her through it.

Kimberly wanted a command in an aviation company more than anything else in the world. She was well on the way to her goal when a hernia popped out on her groin and interrupted her life. I suspected that it happened during the Iron Aviator competition, while carrying the heavy rucksack. The surgeon said the strenuous activity was more than she was accustomed to at any one time. It may have been a weakness Kimberly had since birth, the doctor said, but there was no way to know for sure. One thing was certain: Kimberly needed surgery.

The surgery was scheduled for the end of August, about four weeks after Kimberly started work at the operations shop. She was out of work for about ten days and was on medical profile for several months as she went through rehabilitation and physical therapy after the operation. Her physical activities were limited and she couldn't fly.

As a result, Kimberly was recovering from the surgery at Ft. Bragg and couldn't go to Airborne School to learn how to parachute from planes and become jump certified with other new captains. She watched as others who were jump certified went on jumps and she had to stay behind. She was unhappy with the setback.

Kimberly had hoped to go to Ft. Bragg fully qualified for anything she

An All-American girl, Kimberly enjoys some downtime near home in South Carolina's mountains.

wanted to do. She was ready to jump. It's expected that commissioned officers with the 82nd Airborne have their jump certification. She knew the
missing credential would cause problems later as she sought a command
. . . and she was right.

She also worried that people would think she couldn't carry her own
weight. She was new on the job and already on sick leave and medical profile. Some people constantly have medical problems, and she didn't want
people to get that impression about her, Chief said. So the combination
of being on medical profile because of the hernia and not getting her jump
qualification at this critical time in her career "made it pretty difficult,"
Chief said. "Her main goal was to get healthy as fast as she could and get
back in the S3 shop so she could stand out."

Kimberly worried that others would get a bad impression, but Chief
could tell she wasn't a chronic medical complainer. Hernias happen. He
was there to give her support when she went in for the hernia surgery and
when she got out.

The opinions of others were less generous. Kimberly wasn't jump qualified, she was on medical profile, and she was a woman. A lot of people
thought they'd have to carry her. When Kimberly returned to work after
the surgery, Chief watched with satisfaction as Kimberly overcame her

critics' opinions with her work ethic and won their respect.

Other changes soon began taking place in Kimberly's life. Capt. Will Braman, Kimberly's commanding officer in Korea, returned to the States about three months after she did. He was stationed at Ft. Campbell and they kept in touch by phone, e-mail and an occasional visit. The friendship forged while working together in Korea started to evolve into something more.

"Is there anybody in your life?" Kelli asked Kimberly on the phone. Kimberly, always private and low key about her personal life, said yes, she was seeing someone and liked him a lot. He was good for her, Kimberly told her college friend.

The situation in Afghanistan was never far from her mind. A year had passed since the terrorist attacks on the World Trade Center and the Pentagon and the crash of hijacked Flight 93 in a Pennsylvania field. American and Coalition forces in Operation Enduring Freedom had Al Qaeda and Osama Bin Laden on the run. Afghanistan was the place to be. Kimberly fretted that if her recovery from surgery was too slow, she'd miss out on the action.

That wasn't a problem. Her doctor released her in time to go.

CHAPTER 7

AFGHANISTAN: NOVEMBER 2002

K imberly arrived in Afghanistan at Bagram Airfield two weeks before Thanksgiving, on November 14, 2002. Her home for the holiday season was a compound of tents and trailers in a combat zone, where she was stationed with the Coalition Joint Task Force 180 for Operation Enduring Freedom. The perpetually snow capped peaks of the Hindu Kush rose majestically on the Pakistani border in stark contrast with the flat plain where the former Russian air base was encircled by poverty and war.

The mournful wail of the Muslims' call to prayer lingered in the air daily as people who lived in an adjacent village observed their sacred rituals. Small arms fire punctuated the darkness almost nightly around the perimeter of the base, although few rocket attacks were intentionally fired at the base. Most of the shooting came from local Afghans hunting and, in what seemed to be a common occurrence, locals simply firing shots into the air for no particular reason. Harrier jets, transports, and helicopters flew noisily overhead. There were occasional blasts from planned detonations of explosives by ordnance disposal teams, and every once in a while a land mine was accidentally set off by animals, people or simply time. The dusty air smelled of jet fuel, trash, sewage, coal, and open-air meat markets in the villages.

The base itself was several miles long and about half a mile wide. Thick layers of large crushed rock gravel covered the roads to keep dust down and, more importantly, to make it more difficult for Afghans who worked on the base to plant landmines. Landmines could be as small as a can of snuff, and guards kept a careful watch over the local Afghans who worked on the base. This was war, and the American soldiers could never let their guard down. Kimberly carried either her M4 carbine or her 9mm pistol with her at all times at Bagram, even when she went for her daily run.

The base running track was a dirt road that ran seven-and-a-half miles around the perimeter of the airfield and dead-ended at an airplane graveyard. In dry weather the dirt was like talcum powder and every step stirred up a fine dust. In wet weather it turned to mud and splattered everything.

Kimberly was deployed to Afghanistan because Col. Benny Steagall, the brigade commander, was stationed there and wanted to evaluate her for future command. He liked to handpick his company and troop commanders and took a keen interest in every new aviator captain arriving at Ft. Bragg:

I picked the troop and company level commanders. I size every one up, talk to them, interview them, and approve them before they go into command.

I wanted to know every captain level commander I put in. I knew the war was going to escalate. We were putting captains in charge of troops and pilots, and I wanted them to be very experienced.

She wanted to go to Afghanistan. She was fired up. We were short here and we were rotating folks. I said send her on over here to Afghanistan. We'll work her here and size her up for command.

I had never met her. She arrived, and in our operations center we didn't have any females. She was very attractive. I thought, "Oh, my God." But it was never an issue. As she got into her duties I told her, "You need to jump into some of those CH-47s or Black Hawks." She wasn't in the pilot biz, but in a big aircraft like that you can help out the air crew. It's pretty busy. You need a lot of eyes over there. We just never knew what was going to be shot at us over there. You just never know what's going to come at you.

She went out and toured the fire bases. She came back smiling and gave me a thumbs up. I knew she had what it takes to lead soldiers in war.

She was a pretty quiet person, and she hung to herself. I would see her jogging up and down the road each day. We had to carry our weapons. We had a secure area where we could do our PT. I'd smile at her as we'd pass. She had her 9-mm in her hand. I said, "Yes, she's a serious warrior." Kimberly was the kind of cloth that would have been a senior army leader. She was a trailblazer.

We had a lot of time on our hands and I spent a lot of time with her. She was like a daughter to me. I shared with her an old codger's thoughts about taking care of the kids, the soldiers, being careful and always knowing that the enemy's going to come from where you don't expect it.

Kimberly's first quarters at Bagram were on the second floor of an old burned-out Russian hangar. It was filthy and there was no heat. The climate was much like winter back home in Upstate South Carolina, and nights in the hangar were cold as ice. Soldiers slept on sleeping bags on top of folding cots that were crowded in everywhere, with blankets hung in between them for some semblance of privacy. Learning to change clothes in the blink of an eye on the tennis court paid off now. People were always coming and going, and uninterrupted sleep was a precious commodity.

Kimberly and Major Matt Brady before flying on Christmas Day 2002 in Afghanistan.

Kimberly was night battle captain for Task Force Pegasus of the 82nd Aviation Brigade. She worked twelve-hour night shifts in the aviation brigade's tactical operations center (TOC), a trailer on back of an eighteen-wheeler. It was one of numerous trailers permanently parked around a big aviation hangar. From the outside, the trailer looked like a tan box. Inside, it was a high-tech realm. About eight computer terminals, several sets of regular land-line type telephones, and some sophisticated satellite telephones linked Kimberly and others working with her to the battlefield and to army brass around the globe. A television at one end broadcast CNN and other newscasts around the clock.

Our TOC is kinda like the back of an 18 wheeler. We have an enclosed area behind it with a phone, a fridge, and some game tables. Next to the TOC is a TV tent with a computer that we can use to access the internet, a TV with VCR, a DVD player, and a projector and screen—kinda like a big screen—for movies. Next to the TV tent is the "kitchen tent." It's stocked with food, snacks, personal hygiene items that folks send from the states. Combat these days is very different than it used to be! Now you guys aren't going to feel sorry for me being over here in this third world country!
        —e-mail from Kimberly to Ann and Dale, November 22, 2002

I just didn't dwell on the fact that my precious daughter was in a combat zone. I had to put her wishes and desires ahead of my feelings. Kimberly would have been crushed if she hadn't been able to go to Afghanistan. There wasn't a day that she was gone that I didn't want, from a selfish standpoint, for her to come home and teach English and coach tennis. But I knew she would be miserable doing that until she got ready.

Although it may seem naïve in hindsight, I wasn't nearly as worried about her in Afghanistan, where she had a desk job and wasn't on the front line herself, as I was when she was in Korea flying on the DMZ. I also knew this would be a relatively short deployment compared to the two years she was in Korea. We didn't know exactly how long she would be in Afghanistan, but at the time the deployments typically lasted only a few months, not the twelve to fifteen months seen later in the war.

I was concerned about communications. We had been told that the only way the troops would be able to call home from Afghanistan was to call to a local military line. They couldn't call directly to civilian phones. I worried over the prospect of possibly going for long periods of time without hearing from Kimberly. I saw an article in the Easley newspaper about the local county Veteran Affairs officer going to Afghanistan, and it occurred to me that they might have a military line right there in nearby Pickens, a small town about seven miles from Easley that is the county seat. I called the Veterans Affairs office and asked how the Veterans Affairs officer was calling back there from Afghanistan.

I was given the name of an Army Reserve Center in Greenville that Kimberly could call through. I called them and told them who I was and gave Kimberly the information so she could call home through them.

During the phone conversation, I also learned that the Veterans Affairs officer was stationed at Bagram. I asked the woman at his office if she would give him a message and ask him to look Kimberly up.

Major Rick Simmons, the county Veterans Affairs Officer, arrived at Bagram with the 18th Airborne Corps two days ahead of Kimberly. Rick, who was from Pickens, received my message from his office and e-mailed Kimberly right away: "I'm not sure I've got the right Hampton or not—are you from Easley?"

It was Kimberly's second day at Bagram. She responded, and Rick took a break from work the next night and walked to her office, about three-quarters of a mile down the rocky roads, to meet her.

Rick walked up the steep set of steps at the back of the trailer where Kimberly worked and opened the door, pulling it outward onto the small landing. When he walked in, Kimberly and two other soldiers working inside instantly popped to attention because Rick, a major, was a superior officer. Kimberly flashed her trademark smile and it made a lasting impression. "When Kimberly stands at attention, she beams with that brilliant smile of hers," Rick later wrote of her in a memorial tribute for the local newspapers.

> We hit it off real well. I would see her about once a week. When I'd get the *Easley Progress* and the *Pickens Sentinel*, I'd always take them to her after I finished reading them. She was an only child and I'm an only child. Because you don't have siblings, sometimes you form a relationship in the community that you would otherwise have with a sibling. We would often talk about going to Joe's [a popular ice

Kimberly and Lt. Col. Rick Simmons at Bagram Airfield in Afghanistan.
Courtesy of Rick Simmons

cream and sandwich shop in Easley], and eating. She liked grilled cheese sandwiches and French fries, and of course I wanted my hot dog. We talked about people we knew. She'd tell me about her grandfather who was in the Marine Corps. Her dad was a big football player in Easley High and she and her dad are in the Easley Athletic Hall of Fame. I have a step-sister who's in the Easley Athletic Hall of Fame. We had a lot of stuff in common.

Back home in Easley, it helped Dale and me to know that Kimberly had someone from home who could understand her and where she is from, who could look out for her over there.

"Thank you so much for visiting Kimberly, and thanks too for your kind words and offer of help," I e-mailed Rick Simmons. "Yes, we are very proud of her, and have reconciled ourselves to the fact that she's doing what she loves!"

Kimberly had been at Bagram several days before we received our first phone call from her, patched through from the Greenville Army Reserve Center.

"Mrs. Hampton, I have your daughter on the line."

Aside from hearing your own child's voice on the phone, those were

Kimberly's sleeping area at Bagram Airfield in Afghanistan.

the most wonderful words in the world to a parent of a soldier serving overseas.

It wasn't long until she had e-mail contact, so we didn't have to use the telephone too often. She got a web cam that she could set up on her lap top, and we had a web cam so we could see her and she could see us. There was usually a time delay, so the quality wasn't very good and sometimes the system would hang up, but just to be able to catch a glimpse of her meant so much to us. We had talked on e-mail while she was in Korea, and we had a web cam so she could see us and Tiger, her cat, but we couldn't see her. Being able to see her helped so much. At times I saw excitement in her eyes, at other times I saw exhaustion. Being able to see her sweet face and her beautiful smile meant more to me than words can express, and told me more about how she was doing than words ever could.

Kimberly loved the night shift where there was more action than paperwork. Most combat took place at night and there was some contact almost nightly. As the battle captain, Kimberly tracked everything going on in missions. Kimberly never shared many details of exactly what she did at work with Dale and me. I know she didn't want to worry us. Lieutenant Colonel Mathew Brady, who was at that time a major in command of the 1042nd Medical Company, the air ambulance, described her role as "the eyes and ears of the commander in the tactical operations center when he's not around."

In medevac, we work 24/7. So if we got a nine line—there's nine lines of information that we take for any medevac: type of injury, equipment needed, location, all that kind of stuff - if we got a nine line, then Kimberly would wake me up and then we would go to work. She really became our babysitter, if you will, in that she manned the TOC and we would be out there flying. Her radio operators and her other staff people would be tracking us, where we're going and what we're doing all the way from the time we left Bagram until the time we returned. She became that voice on the other end of the radio that got us home.

Captain Jason King, who grew up in Westminster, South Carolina, about half an hour from Easley, was the day battle captain, doing the same job as Kimberly, but on the day side. Like Kimberly, he flew Kiowas and also was a new captain. They briefed each other twice daily when one came on duty and the other went off:

During your shift you have a plan and track missions as they're going on and let the Brigade Commander know the situation if there's anything going on and what the plans are for the next twenty-four to forty-eight hours. Kimberly and I had to not only talk as far as the job, but we had to be pretty close. We worked twelve to fourteen hours, it depends, because something always happened when you were trying to turn the shift over. We talked a couple hours each day. It was mainly about business, our job. It was pretty stressful being in a combat environment. It was both of our first experience in combat. We definitely put 100 percent into our jobs.

Besides the fact that I knew where she grew up and we flew the same aircraft, I could tell from the first couple of times that I met Kimberly that she was the type of person that I was going to like and that I was going to respect. She was phenomenal. I was very impressed with her professionalism, when she was doing her job, and even when it was just two captains talking.

By Thanksgiving, Kimberly had settled into the routine and had made herself at home in her new surroundings. When Rick showed up at the trailer the night before Thanksgiving with a Thanksgiving card and a care package of near beer, a non-alcoholic brew, she thanked him in an e-mail and by now was comfortable enough to put on her "mother-hen hat" and chide this senior officer in an e-mail for not dressing warmly enough for the walk across the base:

Sir . . . you really must start wearing a jacket when you go out for late night jaunts—it's cold out there! Thanks for making the walk down—know that wasn't easy in the dark! I haven't fallen yet, but I've come very close. Hope you have a great Thanksgiving Dinner tomorrow—I think anything will be better than the standard scalloped potatoes and vege-all!

On Thanksgiving Day, Kimberly, as a young, rising officer, was invited to be part of a group eating Thanksgiving dinner with army chief of staff Gen. Eric Shinseki.

"Not sure he imparted any wonderful words of wisdom, but I was impressed with how he answered questions and addressed issue," Kimberly later e-mailed Rick. "There was no rhetoric . . . just plain talk, which was what we all wanted to hear. We talked about AH-64 tactics, aviation maintenance and maintainers, ROE [rules of engagement] (crossing the PK [Pakistan] border), and the frustrations of depending on the AF [air force] for so much of what we do here."

The dinner lasted about an hour. The occasion "was enlightening, but the food didn't taste great," Kimberly e-mailed Rick. The processed turkey was as far from her mother's cooking as Bagram is from Easley. "I've decided that I might as well just start eating for sustainment, instead of getting my hopes up that the food is actually going to taste good. I spent two years in Korea . . . I'm sure I can handle 4 months of the field DFAC [dining facility, what used to be called the mess hall]. I wanted to lose some weight over here anyway!"

She ate better the next night.

"Major Sexton scored a real live pizza from a Pizza Hut somewhere that the AF flew in tonight. Think it came from Doha, Qatar. There was a little Pizza Hut trailer there. Was nice to have real live pizza again," Kimberly e-mailed Rick. "Think my first meal when I get back will be greasy Papa John's pizza and a cold beer! I'll have to call my parents in advance and have it waiting when I get off the plane! Thoughts like that aren't very comforting over here . . . I try to not think about the food too much. Just makes me want to get home that much more."

Kimberly gave some thought to her future back home as well:

"Would love to have my own helicopter—definitely can't do that on an Army salary, though. Would also be awesome to fly for a sheriff's department, but I suspect I will never have enough experience to even be competitive for a job like that. Usually those jobs go to ex-warrant officers who flew thousands of hours in the military.

"I'll be doing good to just break 1,000 myself," Kimberly wrote in an e-mail.

The Pickens County Sheriff's Office has a helicopter, and probably could use another pilot, Rick told her.

By the middle of December, the relative autonomy of Kimberly's night shift came to an end when Jason's tour in Afghanistan was over and he returned to Ft. Bragg. Taking over the day shift would give her more responsibility and visibility, "but it won't allow me the freedom to come and go as I please during the daytime hours," Kimberly wrote to Rick.

Working dayside, Kimberly was responsible for a lot of briefings. Her day started early with a shift change brief from the night battle captain. Then she had to review any changes that occurred overnight and update several PowerPoint presentations and a fourteen-day calendar of flights in the brigade before she went to breakfast.

Then there were mission requests to review and determine what could and couldn't be supported, and flights to coordinate with the task force in Kandahar. More meetings followed, with the task force at Bagram to work through mission support plans for the next seven days and air mission coordination meetings. Then she met with the brigade executive officer, Maj. Mike Pyott, to see what information came out of meetings he attended and change schedules and coordinate as needed.

Throughout the day she tracked departure and arrival times for all sixty-five Task Force Pegasus aircraft in the country and stayed busy putting out fires and getting necessary information passed along up and down the chain of command. Sometimes late in the shift there was time for PT, but not always. She ended her work day preparing PowerPoint slides for Colonel Steagall's update brief and the shift change briefing. She also prepared slides on the day's missions and upcoming missions for Major Pyott who remembers:

> She got to the brigade right after I moved up to be XO. At that point we kind of knew we were going to be deploying the aviation brigade to Afghanistan, and we were trying to beef ourselves up with personnel. She showed up and we pulled her into the brigade S3 shop.
>
> Normally when someone new shows up, it takes them quite awhile to figure out the unit, to figure out all the procedures and the personality of the unit and of the commander and just generally how things work. Most people show up and they're quiet and subdued and they're looking to see how things function before they really jump in and start putting in a lot of energy into fixing things and trying to improve the unit. Kim was one of those who jumped right in and was figuring things out very quickly and was contributing to a lot of things right up front. That was very key to making sure we were getting all the things done to start deploying the headquarters. She kind of ended up acting as the S3 when the actual S3 was forward. We both went over in November. She went over a couple of days ahead of me because she got stuck in, I think it was Rhoda, Spain, on her way over, and I got stuck in Kyrgyzstan. It was one in the morning when I showed up in Afghanistan, and my body at that point didn't know what time zone it was on. We had spent three days in Kyrgyzstan and then we flew into Kandahar and we caught a flight from Kandahar up north to Bagram. When I walked into the brigade operations center, Kim was on duty. She was wide awake and had a big smile.
>
> "Hey, welcome to Afghanistan, good to see you!"
>
> She had jumped right in when she got there and was already assuming the job of battle captain. Typically the battle captain is the officer who is really running the operations center and in charge of making the on-the-spot decisions for headquarters. It's their job

to determine if they can make the decision as to whether or not something needs to happen or if they need to get the commander or someone with more authority. We place a lot of trust in our battle captains. Some people can do it very well and some people need to have a lot of oversight. Kim was one who immediately jumped in and established herself with her maturity, so they used her as a battle captain immediately.

Kim really became my lead officer in terms of everyday supply and coordinated all the ring routes: basically aviation routes to transport people, equipment and supplies between all the different bases. Everyday there are coordination meetings to determine which route has to be run and what has to be moved. It's almost like a small FedEx operation.

For someone like me and someone like Kim, who's used to dealing with attack operations where you're focused on going and finding the enemy and then shooting them, to deal with moving supplies and equipment and personnel and these logistical type things is very tedious. Army aviation has two sides to it. The attack side, where I'd kind of grown up, and that's all about going out and finding and killing the enemy. The other side of the army is all about moving U.S. forces to go find the enemy and kill them. Kim jumped right in. She took control, and immediately started doing all the coordination for those meetings and running them. I give her a lot of credit, as a young captain, quickly figuring it out. That was her meeting that she ran every day as well as doing the battle captain duties throughout the day in the TOC.

The animated PowerPoint presentations Kimberly prepared showed air mission action across the entire country. She had to produce a lot of different products immediately on request, often within minutes. If she was lucky, she might have an hour or so at the most to produce projects. It didn't matter how difficult the assignment was, she'd look Colonel Steagall square in the eyes and say, "I can handle it, Sir."

Kimberly was "rock solid confident in her abilities and herself," Colonel Steagall said. "She could stand up and brief very senior level officers and didn't show a quiver."

"I stay busy but it's rewarding," Kimberly wrote in an e-mail describing her daily activities to Dale and Ann.

Eventually Kimberly got to move to the canvas tent housing that most soldiers lived in at Bagram. The tents were lined up in neat rows of light tan interspersed with occasional dust-covered olive greens that interrupted but hardly enlivened the drab pattern. The large canvas tents had wooden frames and floors that felt like they were about to take flight themselves whenever the Harrier jets or helicopters passed overhead. Nights were cold, but it was comfortable inside the tents as long as the generators worked.

One of the other captains who enjoyed woodworking made bunk beds out of plywood for Kimberly and some of the others. Her sleeping bag was on the bottom bunk. The top bunk was basically just a plywood shelf where she could keep her belongings off the floor, which was pretty dirty. At the head of the bunk she had a homemade closet with a pole across it where she hung her uniforms. She placed pictures of Will across the top of the closet. At the foot of the bunk she had some shelves.

Most of the soldiers had some type of homemade or locally-made bookcases or shelving that provide storage and a cubicle type wall to separate sleeping areas, and one or two plastic chairs like the ones you'd buy at the Dollar Store back home to put around a back porch picnic table, except these chairs were purchased from a nearby Afghan marketplace. Living in the tents wasn't exactly the Holiday Inn, but compared to the hangar it was the Ritz.

After the hectic workday, Kimberly was part of a group of officers, all captains and majors, who ate dinner together. They walked to one of the two mess halls on the base and took their trays back to the aviation brigade to eat with the other aviation officers and enlisted aviation brigade personnel. "It was like having dinner with your family because everybody always ate together, almost without exception," said Matt Brady, the major in charge of the medevac, who was part of the group. Everyone sat around a giant picnic table and talked and ate barbecue steaks or hot dogs, "whatever we could get our hands on" and shared goodies from home. But the staples were chow hall food: mostly scalloped potatoes, chicken cordon bleu, green beans and salad.

After dinner they often watched television programs taped and sent from family and friends back home in the states. Every Tuesday night they watched *The Sopranos* and every Thursday night after dinner they watched *Band of Brothers*, a story about the army's 101st Airborne Division in World War II.

The episodes were "about thirty days old but to us it was all good," Matt said.

Just before Christmas, the night of December 20, Sgt. Steve Checo of New York, a young man in the 504th Parachute Infantry regiment of the 82nd Airborne Division was killed in battle near the Pakistani border. Kimberly was working when the call came in. Medical and combat helicopters were coordinated and prayers were raised to try to save the young man's life, but later the troops lined up along the road to the airfield and saluted as a color guard and a Humvee transporting the casket passed by. The procession moved by slowly. The troops watched until the casket, an aluminum transport case covered with an American flag, was ceremoniously loaded onto a waiting aircraft and Sergeant Checo began his final journey home.

It was the first time that either Kimberly or Rick Simmons experienced a combat death and they talked about it afterward:

Not that we were there on the scene, but we were both on duty in our respective operation cells, knowing what was going on. As operations officers at night, we're following the battle. Her unit's tracking certain things and where I'm at we're tracking certain things. They don't talk on the radios any more. Everything is on e-mail, like Instant Messages. You can read what's going on and what people are doing, so you can virtually track the battle. You've got a big map showing where everything's at. The call for troops contact comes in, so we know there's a fight going on, then we hear the medevac. They got him back to Bagram Airbase. He'd been shot in the back of the head.

She and I went off duty, and when we went back on duty that night we found out that he'd died. That night we went down to minimum manning in all the operations cells. They had a Color Guard and we all stood at attention. I was there and Kimberly was there. He went by—the transfer case draped with an American flag.

They loaded him up in an airplane and the airplane took off. That was the first guy she and I ever saw killed. We talked about that. It could have been just as easily one of us.

Kimberly told Rick if anything ever happened to him she'd see that his name went up on the War Memorial at the Pickens County Courthouse back home. They talked about seeing that each other would be remembered.

Pickens County has the distinction of having more Medal of Honor winners per capita than any other county in the nation. When the Pickens County Courthouse was expanded in the 1990s, the War Memorial, with a statue and plaques, was built just to the side of the main entrance. Two years later, planning a ceremony and putting Kimberly's name on that monument would be one of the most painful tasks Rick ever faced.

Kimberly had a desk job, so any flying time she managed to get was special. Kimberly and Major Pyott had the opportunity to fly an Apache mission that he said was a highlight of their time in Afghanistan because they got to fly the aircraft instead of just being passengers:

> The danger with most staff [officers] is that we end up getting wrapped into meetings and planning and so forth, and we never actually get out and see what it's actually like to fly in the terrain that we're trying to plan operations in. Normally it's very difficult for someone not qualified in the Apache to fly in the aircraft because it's considered a two-pilot aircraft, so both pilots are supposed to be trained and qualified in the aircraft. I don't know what magic they made work, but we went out and flew with the standardization instructor pilot and I think each of us got about forty-five minutes flying around Bagram and the airfield. We actually got to fly the aircraft instead of being a passenger in the back. That was a wonderful day.

The Christmas season was filled with long days at work for Kimberly, but she was off duty on Christmas Day. Matt knew it was a big deal for her to get away from the base and fly, so he invited her to go along on a medevac mission.

"Think I may get on a flight out to Salerno tomorrow," Kimberly wrote in a Christmas Eve e-mail to Rick. "We have a couple medevac aircraft that are flying out with Warlord 6 and I think they will have an extra seat. Will be kinda like my Christmas joyride!"

It snowed on Christmas Eve and Christmas Day dawned with a light dusting of snow on the ground. There was a Christmas dinner and a Secret Santa gift exchange, but flying with the medevac mission really made the day special.

They flew to Salerno, a forward operating base (FOB) in the Kowst province, about forty-five minutes from Bagram. Thick snow draped the mountainous Pakistani border, but the scene Matt described was no Christmas card picture:

> The mountains are gorgeous, but this is a third world place. The only buildings you see for the most part are mud huts; everything there is just mud. Once in a while you'll see a really beautiful mosque that will really stand out. There's no electricity, they carry water, they build fires in a pit in the middle of their huts, and that's how their families cook and heat and live.
>
> We had gone up there to get a patient, but they weren't ready to come back yet, so we had about an hour to kill. We walked outside the front gates of the FOB and went to the market; these little trailers that the locals have taken over and put all their goods in. [Kimberly] bought a little blue burka, the traditional dress for Afghan women.

The medevac missions Matt flew involved local nationals, particularly children more often than wounded U.S. soldiers. One night after the staff meeting, Kimberly accompanied Matt to the hospital and he walked her through the intensive care unit:

> It tore her up to see kids that way. It hurt all of us. We were constantly picking up children that hit a land mine or were playing with an explosive and it blew up or fire victims, snake bite victims. That really affected Kimberly a lot. It's hard to see that kind of stuff. It's one thing to see soldiers of either side hurt like that because that's

what you expect out of war, but kids don't deserve that. They just got born into it.

New Years was tough for Kimberly, who fought a wave of homesickness:

I woke up not feeling well this morning and just continued to feel worse throughout the day. Drank lots of water and hot tea. Ms. Han used to make me tea with sugar and lemon in Korea when I wasn't feeling well and it always made me feel better. I needed some of that today. . . . Someone had to remind me that today was New Year's Eve. It's just another day here. I have a hard time keeping up with which day of the week it is. If I didn't work with a flight schedule all day, I would really have a hard time keeping up. It's time to start counting the days until I leave now. I'm getting ready to get home. Looking forward to getting back into my old routine, where there is a designated time for PT and I get to come home to my sweet kitty every night. I miss cuddling with her.　　—e-mail from Kimberly to Dale and Ann, December 31, 2002

The perimeter of the Bagram Airfield took small arms fire almost nightly. The Afghans erected little stakes, similar to the stands people use to hold fishing poles along the lakeshore here at home, and launched Chinese rockets from them. Alarms would sound on the airfield and everybody reported to assigned places in three-sided barrier type cement bunkers to wait it out. But toward the end of January, rockets hit Bagram in a more frightening attack.

"We got bombed one night. It was like two or three in the morning," Matt said. "Most everybody was asleep. They sounded the alarm and everybody ran to their bunkers."

One of the rockets landed a yard short of Rick's tent, and another exploded near another tent area. Although they were in a war zone, attacks like this were rare.

"I said a prayer thanking God for the poor gunnery skills of our enemy and for sparing our lives that night," Rick later wrote in a letter to the local Pickens County newspapers.

By the end of January, Kimberly's tour in Afghanistan was nearing an end.

We're finally able to take a breather now that our replacement unit is here. They arrived last week and are now pretty much running the show. . . . Their eagerness is refreshing, as most of my unit has been here longer than me and they are tired and ready to go home. . . . So now I'm enjoying taking naps in the middle of the day and doing a lot of reading. . . . Although I've only been here a short time, working 12 or more hours every day was getting old. I'm ready to get back.

—e-mail from Kimberly to Rick, January 26, 2003

We were ready for Kimberly to come back home, too, but we also knew she loved her work. We worried and we prayed, yet we also knew she'd chosen her own path and found happiness there. As her workload eased and she had time to reflect, she shared her thoughts with us in a February 4 e-mail that we will always treasure because it affirms her joy in the life she chose:

You don't still worry about me do you? Nah! Can't imagine I give you much to worry about. . .I mean, volunteering to go to an airborne unit and jump out of airplanes with only thin material to slow my descent to the earth, and then volunteering to go to a combat zone where there are rockets and gunfights and land mine strikes everyday. Nope. . . . not a thing in the world to worry about. And that's not to mention my chosen profession, which is to fly a single engine helicopter which is overweight, outdated, and slow. No, nothing to worry about!

If there is anything I can say to ease your mind. . . . if anything ever happens to me, you can be certain that I am doing the things I love. I'm living my dreams for sure—living life on the edge at times and pushing the envelope. But, I'm doing things others only dream about from the safety and comfort of home. I wouldn't trade this life for anything—I truly love it! So, worry if you must, but you can be sure that your only child is living a full, exciting life and is HAPPY!

Thank you for always supporting me. I love you.
Kimberly

Kimberly landed at Pope Air Force Base, adjacent to Ft. Bragg, back on Carolina soil late at night a few days later. She was exhausted. She had dark circles under her eyes, which was the dead giveaway when she was tired. Dale and I were standing in a big room at what they call Green Ramp. It seemed to take forever from when we spotted the plane in the distance until it landed on the tarmac. Then the customs officials went on board and it took forever again until everyone came off of the plane. The building was flooded with a sea of soldiers. They all looked the same. We were standing up on benches trying to pick Kimberly out. Finally I spotted that beautiful smile. I think we spotted each other at the same time. We all three had happy tears that she was home safely. As exhausted as she was, she was a beautiful sight to our eyes. It took a little while to get the trunk and bags, so we were all exhausted by the time we got her home, but not too tired to have pizza. We had Papa John's pizza waiting at her house. She reveled in a long, hot shower, we ate pizza and she went to sleep with her kitty. Our baby girl was home.

Kimberly e-mailed Rick a couple days later:

The journey home wasn't bad. . . . We stopped in Turkmenistan, Germany, and Canada on the way back for fuel, so I added three more new countries to my "been there, done that" list. I was able to sleep quite a bit on the flight and it was relatively smooth, thankfully.

My parents were at Green Ramp waiting on me when I got back. Sure was good to see them there! Actually didn't get out of Bagram until late Saturday night (Zulu time). That put us back here late Sunday night (local time). We had a great welcome from the Brigade when we got back.

I'm going through my bags and washing, washing, washing everything. Heading to Easley next week and I will give your dad a call when I get into town. I heard things are heating up again over there. Keep your head down! Let me know if you need anything.

Take care! Kimberly

Kimberly at Airborne School graduation, June 2003 at Ft. Benning, Georgia.

CHAPTER 8

A CAVALRY COMMAND

K imberly hadn't flown a Kiowa helicopter since Korea. The small aircraft weren't used in Afghanistan then because they don't function well in high mountain altitudes.

Kimberly had accompanied a few missions in other aircraft, but for the most part she had been tied to a desk job at Bagram. Now her feet were back on Carolina soil at Ft. Bragg, and her head was in the clouds. She was flying Kiowas again. Dale and I were up in the clouds, too. Kimberly was just a few hours' drive away.

During the day, Kimberly worked for Chief in the aviation brigade operations office, back at the same job she had before her deployment to Afghanistan. Jason King, the day battle captain she'd worked with at Bagram, was also an assistant S3 for Chief, so now they worked together on the same shift. The stress of life as a battle captain in a combat environment was gone, but they were always busy. Cavalry troops were constantly redeploying to Iraq and Afghanistan, and their job was to make sure the troops and equipment all got to where they were going.

JASON KING—

As half the unit was coming home, we were busy sending the other half back over. We were very macro-level planners. We made sure that we had the air force lined up to accept our aircraft and to get our people and our equipment.

We dealt mainly with the air force operation in Charleston getting that set up. Our units that were being deployed dealt with us. So we were basically the middle man between their air force airplanes and the port operations down at Charleston. Our responsibilities were getting our units deployed to Afghanistan and then to Iraq by the air force, by the navy, or by private ship.

In the evenings after work, Kimberly flew, logging hours in the cockpit to demonstrate her proficiency and become current again. The Kiowa Warrior OH-58D, an armed helicopter, is the most sophisticated model of the Kiowa, and Matt Brady, who returned from Afghanistan to Ft. Bragg shortly after Kimberly, admired Kimberly's knowledge of the aircraft:

When you've been out of the cockpit for a certain amount of time, then you have to go back to demonstrate proficiency and take some check rides to show that you can still do the job. And she has to study the aircraft operations book - there's all that studying to do on top of work and on top of flying. When you're away from it you forget stuff, but it's like riding a bike. Your first couple of times on a bicycle after not riding for a couple of years is not necessarily pretty, but you know how to do it. Once you've gotten on that bicycle again and gone a couple times around the block and become real comfortable with it again, then you're fine.

After flying, she always was ear to ear smiling. Flying was everything for her. There was nothing more important to Kimberly than being the best pilot she could be—and she was. She knew that aircraft frontward and backwards.

Aviation is a man's game. It's a good old boy's club if you will, in that it's predominantly male. We're all very A-type personalities. We believe we are the best at everything we do. You have to, to be out flying in combat. You throw a woman into flying, and she's got to be pretty good. She's got to be able to keep up with the boys. But you throw a woman into the cavalry flying 58s, which has forever been an all male club, and she has got to be really good. And that's the caliber of pilot, leader and person that Kimberly was. She could run with any of the guys. Everything she did, she was that good.

This was her world. The spurs, the Stetson, the leather jacket, she played right into this cavalry role - the most difficult job in army aviation, that's what she wanted and that's what she did.

Back home from combat, chow hall food and MREs (meals ready to eat: dehydrated combat rations that replaced the C-rations of earlier times) Kimberly was living on a diet of Chinese food, pizza, ice cream, and sushi. She settled into the house she'd rented in Fayetteville after the Captains Course. She hadn't finished unpacking her moving boxes before she went to Afghanistan, and never did get it all done before she deployed to Iraq. Her day started with PT in the morning with the aviation brigade staff. After work she went to a women's gym and worked out some more before flying. After flying, she studied the aircraft operations book and emergency procedures to review material she'd forgotten while away from flying, while her cat, Tiger, purred in her lap. Dale and I kept Tiger for Kimberly while she was in Afghanistan. I think Tiger was as happy as we were to see Kimberly when we brought her back up to Fayetteville. One day Kimberly told me she'd found a bird's nest in a hanging plant on her porch. She was watching for eggs and babies. Life was good, but the world was about to change again.

U.S. and coalition forces attacked Baghdad on March 20, 2003, a night of shock and awe. It scared me to death to think that this would likely put Kimberly back in harm's way. I never shared those feelings with her. I knew that if she didn't get to go she would be extremely upset, and I just had to accept the fact that she was doing what she wanted to do. I tried not to think about it. I didn't want to act upset in front of her. I wanted to be as strong about it as she was.

For her part, Kimberly was very military and matter of fact and reserved about her feelings on the new Operation Iraqi Freedom when she talked to Dale and me. But she shared her eagerness to serve with friends.

Captain Robin Brown, who crossed paths with Kimberly at Ft. Rucker in the Captains Course, had been in Iraq during the initial invasion. Back at Ft. Bragg a few months later, she heard Kimberly and others discussing rumors that they might be deployed to Iraq. Having been there, Robin wasn't very excited about the prospect, but Kimberly was.

"I'll be the first to go," Robin recalled Kimberly saying. "There was no question that was something she wanted to do," Robin said.

By then Kimberly knew that if she went, she'd go as a cavalry troop commander.

I'm taking command of D Troop, 1-17 CAV. . . You can imagine how excited I am! I am staying busy flying, getting ready for inventories and still working my assistant S3 job at Brigade.
                          —April 24, 2003, e-mail from Kimberly to Rick

Kimberly had approached Lt. Col. Terry Morgan at Ft. Bragg the previous fall before she deployed to Afghanistan and told him she wanted to serve with his cavalry squadron. He was impressed because it's uncommon for a squadron commander to be approached with that kind of request. It's especially unusual from a woman. There are few female troop commanders in the cavalry, an elite, close-knit, traditionally male organization. Lieutenant Colonel Morgan recalled that conversation months later, in the spring of 2003. He was in Kandahar, Afghanistan, and Colonel Steagall contacted him and said he wanted Kimberly to command an airborne cavalry troop.

Change of command was coming up in June for Lt. Col. Morgan's Delta, "Darkhorse," Troop. Kimberly had the qualities he wanted but not the credentials for command. Her missing paratrooper qualification, which had been cancelled due to her hernia surgery, was the problem. According to Lieutenant Colonel Morgan:

> You have to have the right qualifications to serve in my unit because we no-joke go to combat. She's at Ft. Bragg, home of airborne. Ninety percent of the population is airborne qualified. You can't come in and try to lead airborne troopers who have to jump out of airplanes and you not doing it yourself. You've got to do it from the front.
>
> The brigade commander [Colonel Steagall] was saying, "Terry I think she's one of the better of your choices and I want to put her in your squadron."
>
> I said, "Sir, I do not agree with you."

At the same time Kimberly shoots me an e-mail in Afghanistan. "Sir, I would really like to command in the Cavalry. I want to be a commander in your Cavalry squadron."

None of the other captains who were being considered even sent me an e-mail at this point. They're all talking to the big guys, the brigade commanders. I sent her an e-mail back. "You've got to get Airborne qualified first. I have no reservations that you won't go to Airborne School and qualify. I look forward to having you command in my cavalry squadron and I have no doubt you will succeed."

I really put some pressure on her to make her perform at a high level. I was doing it because I knew the battles she would have to deal with and I wanted her to come armed with all the credentials.

Lieutenant Colonel Paul Bricker was in charge of the Kiowa Warrior troops still at Ft. Bragg while Lieutenant Colonel Morgan was in Afghanistan. He'd been a battalion commander in Kandahar while Kimberly was at Bagram. He had seen Kimberly's work in Afghanistan and knew she would make a good commander:

Kimberly was a very effective communicator, whether it's verbal or writing, whether she was giving briefings, she had a knack of being able to quickly cut through the issues, to determine what they were and present that information to the group. Kimberly was one of the more effective communicators for Colonel Steagall.

That's an important trait, especially in the military, because you have to be able to figure out what's important and then what's urgent, and Kimberly had that ability. And she was very approachable. She was a good communicator, she was modest, and she had an affectionate personality. She was a very effervescent officer, so the people enjoyed working with Kimberly.

Lieutenant Colonel Bricker liked what he saw in Kimberly, but he shared the concern about her lack of airborne certification. Because of the heritage and history of the cavalry, airborne certification is a must for 82nd Airborne Division leaders:

That's the 82nd Airborne Division that led the charge in the airborne invasion into Europe in 1944. The 82nd Airborne Division is the point of the spear for America when it comes to putting boots on the ground.

That's the same Airborne Division that Bush 41 [the elder President George Bush] put on the ground when Iraq invaded Kuwait back in 1990. When you're assigned to the 82nd, it's not a matter of if, it's when you're going, because they are America's strategic response force.

She's a female commander now in a group that is heavily male. The paratrooper lifestyle is a rough one. You've got a lot of testosterone in the 82nd Airborne Division. She's leading a group of men who have made a commitment that they want to serve in that unit. You're a double volunteer when you serve in the 82nd. You're a volunteer because you joined the army, and then you're a volunteer to go to the 82nd. You have to volunteer to go to the 82nd. It's a special soldier that says, "I want to be a paratrooper."

I spoke to her a couple times behind closed doors, because these young captains are very excited and eager to assume the role and the mantle of responsibility as a commander. I felt it important as a mentor, as a coach, to be able to talk to these young captains. When you come in as a commander, you are responsible for making decisions that quite frankly can deal with life and death. They are greatly important and you need to have great credibility with your troopers. They need to trust you implicitly because to a large degree, when you deploy in combat, you're entrusted with their lives—the lives of the sons and daughters of our country.

I also wanted to ensure that she understood the importance of being a soldier who made it a priority to know her people, know her soldiers' spouses, and understand as much as possible about each one of those soldiers, because to a large degree she was the mother of those kids. Some of them were older than her, but as a commander, she's in charge of that organization.

It was important that she prioritize her responsibilities to insure that when she took command that she was both mentally and physically ready to go because it's fast and furious. These soldiers are looking at these commanders and they expect complete loyalty, they expect discipline in these organizations to be maintained and they want a leader that they can trust, that they are willing to follow.

I wanted to make sure that I conveyed that to her and that she understood that. She got it. She understood. You could tell. You got that good eyeball to eyeball contact. She asked me very engaging questions that helped confirm to me that she got it.

Kimberly headed to Ft. Benning for Airborne School with mixed emotions. She was excited about taking command but anxious about the three weeks ahead. She had to get through jump school successfully and she couldn't afford an injury.

During the first week of the three-week course students learn about the equipment, work on physical fitness exercises and make jumps from short stands. The second week starts with jumps from 34-foot towers. Students wear parachute harnesses suspended from ropes on a cable and get the feeling of a real jump without falling far. Then they progress to 250-foot towers. Their parachutes are clipped to baskets and they are lifted to the top of the tower and then released while instructors talk them through the landing on megaphones. Most jump injuries occur in the landing, so a lot of time is spent focusing on how to conduct parachute landing falls.

When the third week rolls around it's time for the real thing. Students must make five high performance jumps from jets, land safely and walk off the drop zone before they can graduate.

The first jump is the hardest. As a jumpmaster, Lieutenant Colonel Bricker saw a lot of first jumps:

There are a lot of soldiers doing a lot of praying on the first day of Jump Week. It is really a leap of faith. These kids are in back of an airplane and the airplane is roaring and you're swaying. The aircraft moves back and forth and the jumpmaster opens the door. It's loud. You've got a lot of soldiers packed in the back of an aircraft and they've got all this equipment on, and the jumpmaster's telling them to stand up and hook up, and they start to realize that they're really going to exit an aircraft. Some of them start getting sick.

During those first two weeks, we've taught them all the procedures so it's written in their minds. So when they get into that
aircraft and the door is opened up and the wind is howling through
the aircraft, they pay attention to their equipment and they remember what we've taught them and they follow the instructions of the
jumpmaster as they exit the aircraft.

There are no atheists on that airplane for the first jump. They
are all praying. After they do the first jump, they get a lot of confidence and they are much more aware of what's going on. That first
jump, it's always been the one that I don't think any paratrooper will
ever forget.

The night before her first jump, Kimberly called her college friend
Kelli.

"I'm pretty scared," Kimberly said on the phone.

Kelli had never seen Kimberly scared

"What are you afraid of?" Kelli asked.

"Of dying," Kimberly said.

She asked Kelli to pray for her.

Kimberly and Kelli had compared their beliefs about eternity and an
afterlife in a running conversation over the years, but Kimberly had never
talked about dying, not even when they watched Meg Ryan in *Courage Under
Fire* and Kelli got upset.

They prayed together on the phone. Kelli promised Kimberly she'd
continue to pray.

I was praying, too. And worrying and driving. My baby girl had graduated from tennis serves to jumps from jets. I'd missed only a few tennis
matches, and I certainly wasn't going to miss this. I drove from Easley to
Ft. Benning to be with Kimberly when she made her jumps. I was still on
the road when my cell phone rang. It was Kimberly. She had made her
first jump. Her voice was filled with excitement.

"I'm hooked," she told me.

I was just glad she'd lived through it.

I got to Ft. Benning in time to see Kimberly's remaining four jumps. I
shot video of tiny bodies dropping like rockets in those first seconds after
leaving the aircraft until the parachute opened, and then drifting gracefully

earthward. I never could tell which one was Kimberly. I got to know an army chaplain whose son was jumping, and I leaned on him for comfort as we watched our offspring make their leaps into the sky.

Chief had planned to go to Ft. Benning and make Kimberly's last jump with her, but his daughter, Jenna, was born that day. Kimberly bought a ring for the baby girl to celebrate her birth.

Just wanted to let you know that I completed my last jump of Airborne School last night and I will graduate tomorrow morning. I'm glad it's over! I guess my paratrooping career is just beginning, though . . . I will be heading back up to Bragg on Saturday and my Change of Command is still on for Monday, 16 June at 1000.

— June 12, 2003 e-mail from Kimberly to Rick

Kimberly graduated from Airborne School at Ft. Benning on Friday of Father's Day weekend. Dale and I came to the ceremony and so did Will, who had just returned from Afghanistan. Will got back to Ft. Campbell that Wednesday night and drove to Ft. Benning the next morning, arriving in time to have dinner with us the night before graduation. Kimberly was pretty excited to be done with Airborne School and to have what could have been a career obstacle behind her. She didn't expect it to

Kimberly in formal mess uniform.

be much fun, but her excitement about jumping grew over the three weeks. By the end of the course she was pretty motivated and pretty excited.

The graduation ceremony was held at the Airborne Track, a big outdoor training area in the middle of the post where the stands and towers used in the first two weeks of the course are located. Several vintage airplanes that had flown in the D-Day invasion are displayed at the track, and the new airborne graduates receive their wings in the shadows of those aircraft.

Dale and Will and I sat in the bleachers off to the side of the track with other family and friends of the graduation class of more than two hundred new paratroopers. They marched toward the bleachers in formation singing cadences from the training. When the group came to a stop, the commander talked about what they did during training. Before this day they were "legs" and walked into battle. Now, as airborne troopers they would drop into battle with parachutes.

When the time came for the graduates to get their airborne wings, the formation split apart so families and friends could go onto the grounds and pin on the wings on their uniforms. The three of us walked over to Kimberly and I did the honors, and pinned her wings on.

Even as we performed this rite of passage, Kimberly's mind was already on the next challenge. She was excited to have completed the school but she was looking forward. She was ready to take command.

The two sets of wings on the chest of her uniform, her flight-school pilot wings and the newly earned paratrooper wings, were the outward credentials she needed for that next step, her change of command, which was days away. She would officially take over Darkhorse Troop that Monday at Ft. Bragg.

To celebrate after graduation, Kimberly, Will, Dale and I drove our separate cars in a convoy to our lake house, which was on a small lake nestled in South Carolina's Blue Ridge Mountains. It was Father's Day weekend, and Kimberly gave Dale a Father's Day card, the last he'd receive from her. The message penned in Kimberly's neat handwriting inside, thanking both of us for making this a special time in her life, is among his most valued belongings.

Kimberly and Will left early Sunday for Ft. Bragg so Kimberly could get her house squared away before we arrived. Dale and I arrived that evening and we all went out to dinner and spent a quiet evening together before Kimberly began the next chapter of her life, as a troop commander.

Made it back to the lake house in Tamassee last night after driving through horrible traffic and rain the whole way back from Ft Benning. I'm glad the rain held off for the graduation yesterday. I'm off for another long day of driving back to Fayetteville in just a few minutes.

My boyfriend made it back from Bagram this week and was able to come to GA to see me graduate Airborne school. He'll be at the COC [change of command] as well. I'm thankful for the good timing of these events. . . . Would love to come jump with your unit anytime! I think I've got the "airborne fever" now!
—June 14, 2003 e-mail from Kimberly to Rick

It was a big deal for a female to be taking command of a cavalry troop. Lieutenant Colonel James Viola, who officially transferred the Darkhorse Troop command to Kimberly, had heard good things about her from Colonel Steagall. Less than two weeks earlier Viola had taken over command of 2nd Battalion, and was acting commander of the cavalry troops while Lieutenant Colonel Morgan was in Afghanistan. He liked her attitude. She was serious about her work, fresh out of jump school, and fired up about taking command.

As the morning ceremony started First Sergeant Eric Pitkus, with whom Kimberly had briefly served in Korea, formed up the troopers inside the 1st Squadron, 17th Cavalry, hangar at Simmons Army Airfield. Kimberly, Lieutenant Colonel Viola, and Lt. Brad Tinch, the troop's senior platoon leader who had temporarily commanded Darkhorse Troop while Kimberly was in Airborne School, came forward.

The First Sergeant handed the troop's guidon, a small, red-and-white flag representing the unit, to Lieutenant Tinch, who passed it to Lieutenant Colonel Viola. Then Lieutenant Colonel Viola handed the guidon to Kimberly, officially transferring the command. Kimberly handed it back to First Sergeant Pitkus who carried the guidon back to the formation. Now it was time for speeches.

Following tradition, Lieutenant Colonel Viola talked about the outgoing commander's accomplishments, introduced Kimberly and talked about why she was chosen for the command. Lieutenant Tinch, the outgoing commander, thanked the Darkhorse troopers for their service, and then it was Kimberly's turn. She spoke briefly about her excitement over the new responsibility, thanked the battalion and brigade commanders for the opportunity to lead. She looked toward us and thanked us and all the family.

After the ceremony we attended a catered lunch for Kimberly's soldiers, and our family members and friends who had come to see her change of command. All of my sisters were there, as were some of Kimberly's friends who had taken the time to be with her on this special occasion. There were about a hundred people there. Kimberly was showered with flowers and small gifts. The cake was decorated with a Darkhorse logo drawn in icing from a logo I had enlarged on her computer. Will Braman remembers, "I think what made the day special for Kimberly was having all of her family there."

Will had some time off because he had just returned from Afghanistan, so he stayed with Kimberly the rest of the week but he didn't see much of her. Like all new commanders, she worked long hours. Will had expected that. It wasn't a problem, because that Friday they were flying to Vermont to visit his parents.

Will's father, a retired army colonel who flew helicopters in Vietnam,

Kimberly in red beret worn by airborne soldiers as she gathers her bags
the day she deployed for Iraq.

welcomed Kimberly as "the newest commander in the 82nd Airborne Division." Kimberly first met Will's father in Korea when he came to visit Will and had met his mother briefly at Ft. Campbell a year or so earlier, but this was the first time she got to spend any real time with them. They went hiking in the mountains and to a play. The second day they were there Will took Kimberly to his alma mater, Norwich University, a military college where he received an engineering degree and was in ROTC.

The weather was beautiful during their stay, and Kimberly enjoyed getting to know Will's parents. When Kimberly went to Iraq, she and Will's father e-mailed back and forth about the nuances of being a commander and a pilot in an armed conflict.

Kimberly mentally prepared herself for the day she knew would come, when she would lead her Kiowa Warrior troop into combat in Iraq. She grew quickly in her new role and wasn't afraid to go to her superior officers with questions as she prepared for the task ahead, and Lieutenant Colonel Viola took notice:

> Right off the bat she had a positive and serious attitude. She was serious about her work. She was tactically and technically proficient.

Kimberly and fiancé Capt. Will Braman pose for a picture during goodbyes as she deploys to Iraq.

Her soldiers didn't question whether she knew what she was talking about. You could just see it in her—"Hey, I put the work behind it, here's the plan." I don't know if she ever slept. She was always going. She did all the stuff you see in good leaders, which is listening, paying attention, following when she needed to follow and leading when it's time to lead.

Not long after Kimberly took command, Colonel Steagall returned to Ft. Bragg for his final change of command and retirement. As he walked past his troops for the last time, he saw Kimberly's lips move as she stood at attention in the ranks of officers.

"I won't let you down," she said.

He knew she meant it.

When Lieutenant Colonel Morgan returned to Ft. Bragg from Afghanistan on August 5, 2003, he was immediately notified that he needed to get an aviation task force to Iraq in thirty days. The Darkhorse troop would be one of the units going and things started moving fast.

LIEUTENANT COLONEL TERRY MORGAN—

In the thirty days the commander has to tie up ends and build up confidence in the troops. A lot of emotions are going crazy and she's got to handle that as well as her own. She handled it well.

She had a unique smile, even when times were tough. It had an immediate effect on people and gave them a sense of ease.

One hot, humid August day, Kimberly drove out after work to where Lieutenant Colonel Morgan was watching his son at soccer practice. The sun was still high and the temperature was in the 90s at 6:30 PM; most people would have been happy to stay in an air-conditioned office. Kimberly called on the cell phone and said she needed to bring him some paperwork.

He knew the paperwork was an excuse. She really wanted to talk about the upcoming deployment.

Kimberly arrived in her flightsuit, a one-piece green jumpsuit, and sat on the tailgate of his truck, watching the kids kick soccer balls, and asked his advice on combat and what was ahead.

"I told her I had a lot of confidence in her and everything was going to be all right."

As they talked, his son came out of the soccer game and kicked a ball toward them. Kimberly hopped from the tailgate and started kicking the ball around with the boy on the sidelines and Morgan watched them play. It was one of those moments that always stuck in his mind: she took the time to pay attention to the child. It meant a lot to his son, too. He always asked about Kimberly after that.

As many of you already know, I am deploying to Iraq. Just wanted to pass along my contact information for the next 6+ months:

CPT Kimberly Hampton
D Troop, 1-17 Cavalry
82d Airborne Division
APO AE 09384

I'll send updates as often as possible. Best wishes . . .

                    August 31, 2003 e-mail from Kimberly to family and friends

More than a thousand soldiers were being deployed, taking along fifty-five helicopters and three hundred vehicles. It was time for goodbyes and for beginnings. Dale figured that eventually Kimberly would be sent to Iraq, but not that soon after returning from Afghanistan, but I was in shock when Kimberly called with the news. I knew Kimberly wanted the opportunity to lead troops in combat, and in spite of my motherly concerns, I knew she was following her dream.

Will and Kimberly had decided to get married, but when Kimberly got her orders for Iraq they decided to wait until she returned from Iraq for an "official" engagement. They'd planned to look for a diamond ring for Kimberly's August 18 birthday, , but she postponed the shopping trip until after her return from Iraq. She didn't need to take a diamond engagement ring overseas. Kimberly expected to be in Iraq for up to a year, and Will would head that way himself before long; he had received orders not long after Kimberly to deploy to Afghanistan and from there to Iraq. Although the future was uncertain, they were certain about their plans for a life together.

Dale and I arrived at Ft. Bragg a few days before Kimberly deployed.

She was running on adrenaline, keeping late hours at the office to be sure that everything was ready. Her troop was part of the task force but not part of the battalion they were going with, and Kimberly was preoccupied with last minute details.

Her dining room looked like a bomb had gone off. She had everything she planned to take laid out on the floor so she could survey it before packing. Clothing, personal items, and other gear spilled across the house from her living room to the bedrooms, and office.

Leo, Kimberly's friend from the Captains Course, got back from Afghanistan the day before Kimberly left for Iraq. He was exhausted from the trip but slept little because, like Dale, Will, and me, he wanted to spend every possible moment with Kimberly before she left. The five of us went out to dinner to celebrate Leo's homecoming and Kimberly's departure. Kimberly and Leo knew exactly where they wanted to go: to the Japanese Steak House for sushi.

Dinner was wonderful. I had a lump in my throat the whole time, but I made the best of it. This was supposed to be a fun night. Everyone ate and ate, but the waiter forgot Kimberly and Leo's a la carte order of sushi. Toward the end of the meal the waiter came to the table and asked if they still wanted it. Everyone was already stuffed. Normally we'd have said never mind. But Kimberly was deploying the next day. We waited for the sushi and Kimberly and Leo managed to eat it all. I wondered how they packed it all in.

Kimberly was still packing in the morning and Will helped her while Dale got a bucket of extra crispy Kentucky Fried Chicken and biscuits; I fixed green beans, macaroni and cheese, and sliced tomatoes to go with it. It was a true Southern dinner—the noonday meal is called dinner in the South, followed by supper at night—but Dale wasn't hungry. The lump in my throat the night before must have been catching.

We ate, Kimberly finished her packing, and we loaded up the cars for the trip to a central parking area where the troops were meeting. Kimberly and Will stopped at a hangar on the way to pick up some laptops and went to an ATM machine. Kimberly sent Dale for a pack of gum.

Dale saw tears in Kimberly's eyes as they said their goodbyes, but only for a minute. Kimberly told me she couldn't cry in front of her troops. She was the leader and her troops looked to her for support.

Kimberly poses with friend Capt. Leo Lesch, as he returns from Afghanistan and she leaves for Iraq.

Mom's final hug as Kimberly leaves for Iraq.

Duffle bags and folding cots by an empty aircraft hangar the day Kimberly and her troops arrived at Al Taqaddum, Iraq in September 2003. *Courtesy of Jim Cornell*

Kimberly with Mom and Dad the day she took command of Delta Troop before leaving for Iraq.

Leo knew how she felt inside:

The reality of it hits you. For at least a moment you don't know if it's the last time you'll see your parents. It was good that she had already been to Afghanistan and this was a second deployment. You sit there and look at each other and pray for the best.

I hugged my baby girl, my only child, and tried to pretend she was just going to summer camp. Dale told her to watch over her shoulder and take care of herself, but he had a bad feeling about this farewell. He didn't say anything to anyone else, even to me at the time, but later he said it did cross his mind that this might be the last time he saw her, that this might be their last hug.

Kimberly handled it like a trooper. None of the rest of us handled it very well, but she did.

Dale looked around the parking lot at all the other families going through the same situation. He felt a kinship with these other people, although most were strangers. He knew they felt the same things he felt.

"Daddy, please don't go," a little boy nearby pleaded with his father. The child voiced the words that everyone wanted to say but kept inside.

Dale's uncle had given his life for his country when he was killed in Normandy on June 19, 1944 almost two weeks after having landed on D-Day on Utah Beach. He never came home from war.

With a confident smile on her face, Kimberly headed to the "cattle cars," big trailer-type trucks with seats lining the walls that transported the troops to their departure point, away from their families and loved ones.

They were on their way! Kimberly was thrilled, and it showed on her face. Not going would have been like always going to practice but never getting to play in a tennis match, Kimberly had told us. All I could do was watch her go and try to keep my chin up. I understood what Kimberly was trying to say, but this wasn't just a tennis match or summer camp.

Dale, with camera in hand, chased the cattle car as it pulled away from the parking lot for one last picture. Kimberly wore her camouflage netting-covered army helmet on her head and a smile on her face. Then she was gone.

Kimberly (on left in front row) with some of her Darkhorse troopers in Iraq.

CHAPTER 9

KUWAIT: SEPTEMBER 2003

Thursday, September 4, 2003
No one in their right mind would volunteer to come over here and endure this heat—it's torture! I must be crazy! Ha! I got to fly today—flew aircraft from the port up to Udairi, where we will train for about two weeks before we go into Iraq. It was great to fly, but there's not much to see here. Please tell the Easley folks hello for me when you run into them. I certainly am missing home already. Take good care!
—Kimberly's e-mail to Rick Simmons

Sunday, September 7, 2003
Had a pretty good day. The wind was over 40 knots and at times the sand was blowing so bad that we couldn't see more than 20 feet ahead. Had to break out the goggles to keep the sand out of my eyes. It was bad. Will says he may come to visit you next weekend. I'm jealous—would love to be there too.
—Kimberly's e-mail home

For two and a half weeks Kimberly's Darkhorse Troop trained and practiced maneuvers in Kuwait while guns were mounted on the helicopters. They planned responses to various scenarios, such as loss of communications, aircraft breakdowns or someone being shot down. The pilots worked on brown-out landings in loose desert sand that rose like a cloudy cocoon around helicopters, forcing them to land blind. They flew maneuvers in the dark with night goggles and completed training drills that were required before they would be allowed to cross into Iraq.

Three instructor pilots served with Kimberly's troop: CWOs James "Willy" Williamson, Jim Cornell, and Lee Conley, who was the senior instructor pilot. Only Willy and Jim were initially assigned to the troop, but because it was a young troop, Jim asked for a senior flight instructor to assist them. Lee was assigned to the troop shortly before they left Ft. Bragg. All three were experienced combat veterans and it was their job to prepare the pilots for the rugged flying conditions they would face in the desert.

JAMES "WILLY" WILLIAMSON, instructor pilot—

The closest reality we have to Iraq is in Kuwait. It's a good place to practice without having someone looking for you to gun you down.

DONOVAN McCARTNEY, pilot—

Most of us were pretty scared. We knew we were flying into combat. We had some veterans from previous wars but none of us had been into Iraq. It was definitely an unnerving experience because we didn't know what to expect. We didn't know if as soon as we flew over the border into Iraq if we were going to get shot at or if people would be waving at us.

Kimberly was responsible for sixteen pilots, including herself and her two platoon leaders, plus eight mechanics, a first sergeant and about $25 million worth of equipment and aircraft. She did her homework and was confident and in control. Her soldiers never saw the burden of command, the toll on her, but as a mother, I could feel it. I could read it between the lines in some of her e-mails home.

The 120-degree Kuwait heat and stress of anticipation wore nerves thin. Personality conflicts between some of the soldiers bubbled to the surface. Kimberly confronted those conflicts head on and got everyone settled down so they could work together effectively. Donovan McCartney liked the way Kimberly treated people and the way she tapped the various talents and skills within the troop to benefit everyone:

She would talk to you like you were a person and an equal, as opposed to ordering you to do something. She led from the front.

She was right there next to you. She never delegated the jobs that were hers to someone else.

She wasn't necessarily the most experienced aviator. She only had four or five years of experience, but some of the guys around her had fifteen years of experience. She was kind of the orchestra leader and she would try to direct the information out of the people that did have it toward the people that needed it. She was always good at asking questions, and I think she used her inexperience to help draw information out of some of the experienced guys so some of the inexperienced guys could use it. We were always sitting around and talking and having guys tell stories about things that happened before so we could all learn as much as we could from other guys' experiences.

Kimberly was earning the respect of her troops, but she did take some flak during the stressful time in Kuwait as the soldiers made the adjustment from life back at Ft. Bragg. At the end of each day, when she released her troops in standard military form with the words, "You are dismissed," she received increasingly sarcastic responses. It wasn't like they could go home to wives and children and relax. Being "dismissed" meant little in Kuwait. They couldn't do the things they wanted to do. One day when it was time to dismiss the troop Kimberly looked up and down the line of soldiers.

"You are released to manage your own time," she announced.

They got the message.

It became her standard dismissal for the Darkhorse troopers in Kuwait and in Iraq.

Greetings and salutations to the families of D Troop, 1 Squadron, 17th Cavalry Regiment. The Troop is currently residing at the scenic Camp Udari in North East Kuwait. The camp is everything one would expect from an exotic Army vacation hot spot. The amenities and attractions include tents for 70 personnel, running water . . . sometimes, daily sandstorms, temperatures averaging 120, and electricity provided by a large generator situated 25 feet from each tent.

Despite how primitive this might sound, the Troop is performing at top form. We have begun our training in preparation for the move north into Iraq, by conducting operations in sand and dust clouds as well as an aerial gunnery event. The crew chiefs

Kimberly on duty in office built by her troops in Iraq.

are working hard day and night to ensure the Troop's aircraft are at the highest state of readiness.

The morale in the Troop is very high with the expectations of assuming our mission in Iraq. The camp offers daily movies, a great gym, and an endless supply of ice cream to keep our spirits up while we are here. Your e-mails, letters and support of your family members are the best way to keep us focused and remind us what we are truly fighting for.

—Kimberly's newsletter to her soldiers' families back home

The ice cream freezer in the dining facility was first stop for the troops when they came in for lunch and for dinner. It was their oasis after long hours in dust and desert sun. Premade Kuwait-style, Nutty-Buddy type ice cream cones, wrapped in packages covered with Arabic writing, were "pretty much the only cold thing we could get our hands on," said Adam Camarano, one of Kimberly's two platoon leaders.

As the troops endured Kuwait and anticipated Iraq, they also were assessing their new female commander. Chief Warrant Officer Lee Conley was assigned to Kimberly's troop about two weeks before deploying, so

Kimberly carries a lunch and some homemade cookies from friends to work in Iraq.

they didn't have a whole lot of time to get to know each other before arrival in Kuwait:

> We were still trying to figure each other out. Here I am, the new guy in the troop who she doesn't know and I'm supposed to be her senior advisor. It's a tough role.
>
> She'd been in command only a few months. We had some good talks and she seemed to have a good head on her shoulders, had a lot of good common sense and trusted a lot of the experienced people around her. She had the command presence and was going to make the decision and was going to do the right thing. She wasn't afraid of being in command. She wasn't afraid of commanding mostly males, which is kind of difficult in the military sometimes. We were extremely busy in Kuwait. Myself, Willy, and Jim were doing a lot of flying—doing what they call environmental qualifications. She was busy doing her thing as a commander and I was busy doing my thing as a trainer, but we did get together on several occasions and talk.

Lee always called Kimberly "Thirty." He gave her the nickname when she fussed at him over her age on her birthday a couple of weeks before they deployed.

"I'm not thirty. I'm twenty-seven," Kimberly retorted.

"That's close to thirty," Lee responded and that's what he always called her after that.

At six-foot-three and more than two hundred pounds, Lee was a large man. When he and Kimberly flew together he always noticed the contrast in how much space each took up in the cockpit.

While she was comparatively small in stature, Kimberly made it clear that she could pull her own weight in terms of physical strength and needed no help. She wouldn't allow anyone to do anything for her just because she was a woman, Jim said. One particularly dark night, Kimberly, Jim, Brad Tinch, and several other pilots, who were all large men, were walking from the flight line to the tents about half a mile away. Each of them carried thirty or forty pounds of body armor, publications, and other flight gear, and they offered to help Kimberly but she wouldn't let them. There wasn't much of a path over the rough and rocky terrain, and suddenly Kimberly toppled over under the weight. As the men scrambled to help her up, Kimberly looked at them from the ground and started laughing. It was contagious and soon they all were laughing. Kimberly got back on her feet, dusted herself off, and grabbed her gear back from a couple of the men who had picked it up, and they all laughed even harder. Kimberly and her officers were still laughing when they got to the tents, and for a few minutes they forgot the stress that was building as time to cross the border to Iraq drew near.

One time Kimberly broke her self-imposed do-it-herself rule; she asked Jim's help with a complicated helicopter landing being filmed by a news crew. Kimberly was one of two female unit commanders in the aviation brigade and some embedded reporters in Kuwait wanted to interview them. It was the day Kimberly was scheduled to do her brown-out training with Jim. The training was done away from the airfield because the landings kicked up so much sand, so the reporters asked Kimberly to do a brown-out landing between the runways at the airport when she flew back in from the training, then get out of the aircraft and walk to the cameras for the interview.

Kimberly was more than competent as a pilot, and did her landings well, but as she and Jim flew back toward the airfield, she asked Jim to do the landing there for her because she was nervous about the filming and wanted it to be perfect.

"Ma'am, you've just done five good landings," Jim said.

Kimberly thought about it.

"Okay," she said.

Her landing was good. Kimberly jumped out of the aircraft, smiled into the rolling cameras, and walked to the appointed spot for the interview that later aired on ABC. Landing a helicopter in the blowing sand and dust is like having "a brown paper bag over your head," Kimberly told the reporter. "You can't see much at all."

Jim was still shutting the Kiowa down when Kimberly bounded back across the airfield after the interview. "Thanks for not letting me wimp out," she said.

In the final days before crossing the border, Kimberly and the three instructor pilots considered the potential threats ahead and plotted their strategy for the flight to Al Taqaddum, where they would be stationed in Iraq. They staged a rehearsal the day before they left.

LEE CONLEY—

The time for training was over. It was like a football game going into fourth quarter. I'm the type of guy, I plan for the absolute worst and hope for the best. Kimberly was kind of the same way. We planned for the absolute worst going inbound, as far as weapons configurations, where the experienced pilots are in the formation of the aircraft, who flies with who, and all the plans: If we get hit inbound what are we going to do, and things like that. We went through it very extensively.

Almost everyone was nervous. Kimberly prepared a final briefing and asked Willy, Jim, and Lee for their thoughts on what she should say to her troops.

"Don't lie to them," said Willy, who had previously served in Bosnia with U.S. Air Force Special Operations and knew what it was like to take fire.

"Tell them how it's going to be and tell them the reality. Tomorrow's for real," Willy told her.

The solemn briefing "was probably the pivot of getting everybody together on the same sheet of music and having everybody together in a tight bond," Willy said.

Wednesday, September 17, 2003

We are in Kuwait for just a couple more days. We have been busy, busy . . . doing environmental qualifications, gunnery, small arms ranges, classes and maintenance. My challenges as a commander continue to grow and change . . . It is truly an honor to be a Troop Commander in combat. I sent guys forward on the ground today. I'm certain that I will never forget the feeling I had when I saw that convoy roll away. Tough to describe over e-mail—heck, tough to describe, period. Felt a lot of different emotions. I'm sure that the day we cross the border in the air will be similar for me.

Thursday, September 18, 2003

Only have one more night after tonight before we head north. We're doing a lot of planning and rehearsals, preparing for the flight. Our guys on the ground have already started their movement. We have heard the news reports, but don't know if our guys were involved. It's hard not knowing what's going on with them.

—Kimberly's e-mails to Rick Simmons

As the ground crew drove into Iraq with the trucks and supplies, an Iraqi vehicle rammed into the back of one of the trailers they were hauling and damaged it so badly that it had to be left behind. The trailer was carrying cots, tents, and other materials for their living quarters. The contents were saved and moved to another vehicle. No one was hurt except for the Iraqi. The Americans didn't know whether it was intentional or not. They kept moving, following strategy they had practiced in Kuwait, to avoid being caught up in a crowd of Iraqis as people gathered at the scene of the wreck.

Kimberly and the other Darkhorse pilots heard the news by word of mouth but didn't know if the incident involved their troop or another.

JAMES "WILLY" WILLIAMSON—

It was frustrating, I imagine for her—her first event as a commander and she's not even with her guys.

When Kimberly arrived in Iraq and got the details, "she was happiest that no one was injured," Adam said. "The equipment damage was secondary to the well-being of her guys."

I had several long Instant Messenger chats with Kimberly in the last few days before they flew into Iraq. She had sent her sleeping bag forward and was spending cold nights wrapped in a poncho.

So you're going Sat?

Yes.

Have your guys arrived there yet?

Some of them have, some have not—still on the way.

Do you know your route when you go up? How long will it take?

Yes, I know the route—about 5.5 hour flight.

Can you tell me how you'll go? Or not?

Can't say. Pretty straight route though.

Do you have anything to help keep you warm tonight other than your poncho?

Another guy let me use a poncho liner. I will sleep in my uniform tonight.

That's amazing . . . burn up in the daytime and freeze at night.

Yes, but it's about 80 at night—weird, huh? The days are around 110.

I guess it's the temp swing that makes it seem so cold at night. Are you able to go to bed at a reasonable time tonight?

Yes, we are finished planning for today, so my night is free! (unless the col calls a mtg.)

Do you think there will be any way you can call before you leave Kuwait? I sure do hope so. But just in case, just remember that we are right there with you every mile of the way. Actually I guess I'm glad that you're flying rather than riding in a convoy . . . never thought I would say that!! Hope your mtp [maintenance test pilot] is in his top flying form! And you get lots of rest so you will be sharp too. Wow, I just can't imagine the experiences you're going to have. You're going to see lots more than you want to, and will see lots that you want to forget. Maybe you can remember the good experiences, the lessons learned, the poor people who have been liberated, and that you've done (more) your part to help make this country a safer place for those who love you. Well, sweet girl, I'm sure you're tired of reading now so I'll shut up!! I hope to talk to you either online or on the phone, but if you don't get a chance to do either, just remember how much you're loved and respected and take it one day at a time, while looking forward to a wonderful future! I love you darling, mommie

We talked online again later.

How do you feel about moving up north?

Ready to go, I guess. That's why we're here.

How are your guys? Is everyone in good shape?

They are okay—we're having ups and downs, but we'll be alright.

Do you have anyone you can hang out with?

Yes, I hang out with my guys, or with the other commanders. Have lots of CPT friends here.

We talked about the cats. Kimberly could see them playing on the web cam. I forwarded her a copy of the televised video taken during the training in Kuwait and she watched it.

Hey—that was awesome! I didn't look dumb! My hair wasn't messed up either!

Of course you didn't look dumb! It did us so much good to see you laugh! And it wouldn't have mattered if your hair was messed up. It was windy, after all!

Great.

Yeah.

Well, I'm going to head to bed.

Okie sweet girl. Is everyone going up Saturday?

Yes.

Are the blackhawks there?

Yes.

Will y'all go up together?

We will go separately.

Well, will talk to you tomorrow, okay?

I'm sleepy.

Okay my sweet girl. Get a goodnight's rest now, okay? I love you very much. Sweet dreams.

I love you too. Goodnight.

We chatted online twice the next day. She had spent a cold night sleeping in her uniform. I told her she needed her cat, Tiger, there to snuggle with, and she agreed. I know she missed Tiger and she always enjoyed seeing the cats playing over the webcam. She had just had lunch, pork chops and ice cream, when we talked the first time that day, and she was going to wash all her clothes before leaving Kuwait. Water was rationed where she'd be in Iraq, so she knew she wouldn't be able to wash often.

We got to IM-chat online one last time before she went to bed.

I'm sending you kisses.

Thank you—sorry to make you sad.

I just want you to be safe and happy baby.

I will be both—don't worry.

I've got lots and lots of faith that you will be. You've got some angels on your shoulders!

I know. Sure do.

Is everyone settling down for the night? It's after 11 there, right?

Yes, everyone is getting ready for bed. Not too early of a morning tomorrow.

Well, I hope to talk to you soon, baby girl. I'll be thinking about you all the time, and hoping and praying that all goes well for you and your guys. Keep a good attitude and remember how much we love you. Just think . . . almost three weeks is gone already!!

I know . . . time will fly by. Thank you for your thoughts and prayers. I love you very much and will write often. Be safe. I love you!

I love you very much and can't wait to see you. If they open up Baghdad international, I want to come over!

No way! Too dangerous! Okay—goodnight. Love you! Bye!

Goodnight baby. Be safe and happy . . .

I will.

I love you baby girl . . . be safe and happy!!! mommie.

25/12/2003

Kimberly celebrates Christmas 2003 in Iraq.

CHAPTER 10

IRAQ: SEPTEMBER 2003

T he eight-hour flight from Kuwait to Al Taqaddum, an abandoned
airfield west of Fallujah in central Iraq, was smooth and uneventful.
At one point during the flight, some of the pilots saw mirror
flashes from shepherds in the desert. Some of them thought they were
muzzle flashes from a gun. Everyone wanted to turn in that direction, but
Kimberly kept them focused on the mission and didn't let them get side-
tracked.

LEE CONLEY—

*Flying inbound, even though everybody's apprehensive, you're excited to go. If
you just went to football practice every single day and never got to play in the
game, you'd eventually get tired of going to football practice. I'm not saying
anybody wishes for war, you don't, but it's happened, it's time to go, this is what
I've been practicing for. Everybody wants to practice their skills. The problem
is every little thing might be a bad guy and everybody wants to be the first one
to see it. She was real aware of that. She'd reel everybody back in, and say,
"Hey, let's concentrate on what we're doing and let's get to where we gotta go."
I think it went fairly well for the first flight in.*

DONOVAN McCARTNEY—

It was a pretty long day. It was like seven or eight hours. We left Kuwait and flew across the desert, off in the middle of nowhere, for like two hours and you didn't see anything. Our first refuel stop we landed on a highway. Military police shut off traffic in this highway and we set up a big refuel camp right in the middle of this highway. We left from there and we flew to Talil, a United States Air Force base. It was an old Iraqi airbase that we had taken over. We flew to there and refueled, which was nice, because when we refueled on the highway, we didn't have anybody guarding—we had to fly around and guard ourselves. When we landed there, it was a secure air base that had a perimeter and everything. It was a whole lot better than being out in the middle of nowhere."

Al Taqaddum, TQ for short, was also called Forward Operating Base Ridgway by the Americans at the time. The base was enormous. The runway alone was a couple of miles long, but there wasn't much infrastructure left after the Americans bombed it in the first Gulf War.

DONOVAN McCARTNEY—
When we first got there, there was nothing there. Before the 82nd got there, people had stayed there just temporarily, but we moved in to basically just a sandbox. We had to clean out our own hangar in the building and get all the trash out of the way and there were old Iraqi airplanes blown up all over the place we had to move out of the way. They had toilet facilities, but not much. There was like one toilet for like every hundred people.

The only showers were a long way away, but it had been a long day. Kimberly and Lt. Jen Leidel, her senior platoon leader and the only other woman in the troop, were ready to wash off the dirt and sweat. They asked for directions and one of the guys who had arrived a day earlier pointed off into the distance. Kimberly and Jen headed off into the night.

The hulks of ghostly aircraft were scattered here and there. There were a lot of roads but no indication of where they went. Kimberly and Jen walked and walked and suddenly noticed little plastic orange surveyor-type flags stuck in the ground in front of them. Jen recalled:

We both had these crummy flashlights. They weren't very bright. So I stopped. I said, "What's that?" and she said "It's a landmine," because in the briefs we had gotten, that's how they marked land-mines.

We stopped and we're both a little nervous. We look around and we shine our lights and we're surrounded by them. They're in every direction. They're behind us, they're on both sides, they're in front of us. We look further and three sides of us are surrounded by a chain link fence with barbed wire around the top.

We ended up turning around and going back the way we came in. We walked really light because, I don't know, in our heads I guess we thought the land mines wouldn't go off.

We finally make it to this road. We keep walking in the direction we think we have to go and we see some guys sitting there. They were army engineers.

"Do you know where the showers are?"

"They're down that way"

"Do you know what all these flags are behind the building?" Jen asked.

"Yeah, that's where we're going to put up your tents."

I could have sworn that we decided at that point that we weren't going to tell anybody that story, but by the time I got back to the tent everybody knew the whole story. I think she told them because she thought it was funny.

For the first week or two, the soldiers slept on cots next to the vehicles or inside a sand-covered concrete dome aircraft hangar with open ends that had been built by the Iraqis before the airstrip was abandoned a decade earlier.

Their first job was to make the place livable. Old, blown up Iraqi airplanes had to be hauled out of the way. They set up a mobile kitchen and ate their meals under what looked like a circus tent.

They built a makeshift solar-heated shower near where the Darkhorse tents would be. Willy and Jim rigged up a steel frame they found in an old trash pit. It looked like it might have been stairs or scaffolding at one time. They piled plywood around three sides and hung a poncho across the front. They filled a five-dollar camping shower bag Willy had brought from home, "just in case," with water from five-gallon cans and let the scorching desert sun heat the water. It was primitive, but it worked and it was close by.

DONOVAN McCARTNEY—

That was the best thing in the world, coming back after a long day and knowing you had a shower.

A long building was designated for troop offices. Jim and Willy found carpentry work was a way to escape the stress and threw themselves into building walls around the approximately ten-foot by twelve-foot space for Darkhorse Troop. They constructed a U-shaped shelf all the way around the walls, picking a random height for the countertop. They were tall men and it was a little too high for Kimberly. When she sat in the folding chairs they had in the office, the shelf was almost up to her armpits.

JIM CORNELL—

As a joke we built her a booster seat. We spray-painted it in red and white, the Cavalry colors. We labeled it "Darkhorse 6." [Six is the traditional call sign for a unit commander.] We built it as a joke, but she actually used it.

Someone scrounged up an old air conditioner for the work area. They also found an old heater that went unused during September's 100-degree days but was welcome when night temperatures dropped in the winter months.

While Kimberly and Jen worked on getting the headquarters office set up, Adam worked with the aircraft mechanics, who were constructing a small building for their tools and equipment where they could work on the helicopters. Kimberly enjoyed learning about the maintenance operation and would ask questions but didn't micromanage.

"She let us do our job, and then if we began to stray a little she would rein us back in," Adam said.

Initially life was tense, recalled Mac, Kimberly's friend from Camp Stanton in Korea, who was also at Al Taqaddum with the 82nd Airborne, but before long everyone settled in to a routine. "Once you get used to where you are and the living conditions it becomes normal, so you revert to your normal self," he said.

D Troop has finally settled into a routine here at TQ. We spent two weeks planning and conducting missions during the day and night. We are now on the Quick Reaction Force (QRF) to respond to short notice missions. So far we haven't been needed for that purpose, but we have been conducting daily reconnaissance throughout our area of operations.

The crew chiefs put a great deal of work into their crew "shack" where they work and five of them sleep. They added on an extra room for sleeping and they are currently working with C Troop to build another room for a television. They are also enjoying nightly games of beating C Troop in kick ball.

. . . The facilities here keep improving and we hope to see a Dairy Queen in the near future. This is wishful thinking of course, but ice cream is the number one luxury we all would like to have. So think about us and dedicate your next cone to the brave Troopers of the mighty D Troop, 1st Squadron 17th Cavalry regiment.

—Kimberly's October 15, 2003 "Darkhorse News"
to families back home

The frame tents the Darkhorse troopers brought with them to Iraq were set up on a cement slab behind the hangar. They were lucky to have such a good spot. Other units had tents that were directly on the sand and were plagued by sand fleas.

Darkhorse pilots connected two side-by-side tents to create one long tent, but it was literally and figuratively a world away from the aviators' hallway back at Ft. Leavenworth. Each cot was about two feet from the next one, with just enough room to walk between them. There was no privacy, it smelled, and with that many men living that close together it was pretty much of a mess.

It was like living in a men's locker room, but when Kimberly and Jen were offered space in segregated female quarters they declined because they wanted to stay with their soldiers. Kimberly always kept her own little space tidy and organized. All her socks were rolled up neatly and Jen noticed that when Kimberly got out her clean clothes to put on after a shower, everything was always folded and very organized. Every night before she went to sleep, Kimberly would sit on her cot and take her long, curly hair out of the tight bun and pull the brush through it peacefully and calmly like a cat taking a bath in the middle of surrounding chaos.

October 24, 2003
We kinda live in a ghetto right now—crowded with clothes and equipment hanging everywhere. Everyone is pretty comfortable, though.

   All in all, it's not too bad here. Would much rather be at the lake, but I can handle some time here temporarily.   —Kimberly's e-mail home

Kimberly was happy to be doing something "real," instead of training and simulations. She was learning a lot and enjoying the flying. "Overall this is a great experience and I wouldn't trade it for anything," she wrote to us, but when it came to living conditions, I believe she was looking on the bright side. They were the worst Willy said he had encountered in his seventeen years in the military.

Winter rains flooded the tents with ankle-deep water on the ground for weeks at a time and the soldiers nicknamed their tent "Lake Darkhorse." Running shoes and anything else left on the ground under the cots floated around the tent, adding to the disarray. Everyone scrounged for pallets to keep their belongings out of the water.

They lived out of rucksacks and big plastic footlockers from a previous deployment to Bosnia. When the tent flooded, everything was piled on the cots until it was time to sleep, and then moved to the tops of the footlockers or dumped on fold-up camp type chairs. Any scrap wood that could be found was made into shelving to keep things off the ground. Jim built some shelves over his footlockers and then built six or eight sets of the shelves for some of the others. Donovan built a bed frame with shelves underneath the mattress. He set the whole thing high up on pallets and everyone called it "The Ark." Kimberly described the living quarters in a November 16 e-mail to us:

It's kinda like a scene from a Vietnam movie. We've sandbagged most of the tents and it's like a little village or something. Clothes hang on the line between the tents.

Sometimes Kimberly ran in the mornings, but she had to fit her schedule around flying, so she often ran later in the day. A two-mile route led from the area where the Darkhorse tents were to a spot on the base called "Wings," where some soldiers had taken the rear wing tips from an old

Iraqi jet and dug them into the ground. It was the turnaround point for Kimberly and others from her area of the base when they were running. As she approached the wings, she always kept an eye out for Joel Crawford, who lived in one of the tents near the wings and was from Clinton where she'd gone to college.

He called her "home girl," and it always made her smile.

Joel had met Kimberly at Ft. Bragg when she returned from Afghanistan. The first time he saw her he took notice because he'd never seen a female commissioned officer with crossed cavalry sabers on her collar before. The second time he saw her she was in her car, with South Carolina plates, and he stopped her to find out where she was from. When she said Easley, he told her he was from Clinton and she told him she'd gone to Presbyterian College there. He started calling her home girl after that. They'd both deployed to Iraq, and although he worked and lived two miles from her on the base, he saw her often in the mess hall and around, and she always gave him a smile and a wink. Sometimes he saw her in the mornings when he ran, but because she had to run around her flight schedule, he usually would see her running later in the day and would wave as he drove by.

The 82nd Airborne had five aviation units on the base, two air cavalry troops and three helicopter companies. FOB Ridgway became a mini-tent city as life settled into a structured military routine. The five groups separated into shifts, with four units flying and the fifth unit on standby while maintenance work was done on their aircraft. They worked twelve-hour days and flew daily for eight weeks except when grounded by weather, and then rested for two weeks on standby. Kimberly told us a little bit about it in her October 24 e-mail:

> We have kinda adopted the philosophy that if we are flying, then we are deterring enemy action, so we try to stay in the air as much as possible. Will be especially critical as we transition to the night shift. The bad guys come out at night. They are leaving our camp and the aircraft alone for the most part. They are hitting the ground guys hard. IEDs are the biggest threat and they are everywhere. We spend most of our days out hunting for them or for the guys who look like they are emplacing them.

The proficiency and frequency of IED (improvised explosive device) attacks in Iraq were increasing, with many attacks directed toward U.S. and Coalition convoys. A good number of Iraq highways are extensive, modern, four to eight-lane paved roads, and the enemy often emplaced the explosive devices in the built-up or vegetated medians by burying them in holes or concealing them along guard rail girders.

The battalion commander, Lt. Col. Spencer Artman, commander of Task Force Wolfpack, emphasized the importance of continued reconnaissance in order to find the insurgent forces planting the IEDs and directed the pilots to keep a presence on the division's main routes:

> Later as our knowledge of the area and enemy tactics increased, we were able to draw a direct correlation between the number of these incidents and the frequency of our reconnaissance efforts.

Darkhorse troop flew its first combat mission just days after they arrived in Iraq. Before the mission, Kimberly, Lee, Jim, and the task force operations officer went to a rehearsal with an infantry unit across the river from them before the mission. The colonel conducting the rehearsal was going over the timeline for the early stages of the mission. He looked at Kimberly and said, "What are you doing at this point?"

It was Kimberly's first time in the spotlight in a combat situation. She carefully went through every detail of the air support plan. When she finished, the colonel just chuckled. He only wanted to hear what aviation was doing at that particular point in the timeline, not the entire plan, he told her.

Kimberly was embarrassed. Jim could tell and gave her a thumb's up to encourage her. She'd told the colonel more than he wanted to hear, but her explanation was "absolutely on the money perfect," Jim said.

When they flew the mission the next day, they found the guerrilla-style activity was quite different from anything they studied in training. There were no frontlines. The enemy was all over.

Afterward, Kimberly and the three instructor pilots mulled over the information and options.

JIM CORNELL—

It was always a collective effort. There's so much out there that no one person knows it all. We came up with a technique—not just the troop but as a task force. You do it at a task force level, too. All the different units figured out the same thing, so it kind of validated what we figured out. It's such a fluid place. It's such a dynamic battlefield, we have to constantly adapt to it. Each mission had its own individual details that you had to work out. When we got over there, we had a pretty good idea of what we wanted to do as far as how we were going to work it, and for the most part it was effective, but we underestimated the bad guys. We discovered that pretty quickly, so we had to start adapting immediately.

The first time Jim and Kimberly flew together in combat was a night mission chasing after the secretary to Chemical Ali, a notorious figure in Saddam Hussain's regime:

She just jumped right in with both feet. Usually as an instructor I'll go out with the person I fly with afterward and kind of debrief them. Part of my job is training and standardization. Making sure everybody operates similar enough that they are standardized and point out places where they can improve efficiency-wise or anything. After that flight with her, that first combat mission I flew with her in the cockpit, I really didn't have anything to say other than, "Good job."

A lot of commanders are hesitant to get out there, especially with the senior people, because they're afraid of their senior people realizing they're not as proficient as they should be or as they want to be. I never had that problem with her. She never passed up an opportunity. She led by example and was very good at it.

Probably one of the hardest things for them to handle is being in charge of the flight. They take the brunt of the radio traffic. We have four different radios in the aircraft, and when they're all going at the same time it can get challenging. She was like an old seasoned pro.

That's one of the more relaxing things, when I get to fly with someone who is that proficient. I don't have to pick up any of the slack. As a general duty, the person flying the airplane in the right seat, that's their primary responsibility, just flying the airplane. The person in the left seat is the one that handles the mission stuff, the radios, the sight, all the other stuff. With her I got to just sit there and fly.

Before long they were chasing Saddam himself. Jen's team was out on standard patrol and Jim and Kimberly were on the team waiting to relieve them when a call came in that Saddam was at Ar Ramadi, a hotspot that was one of the bastions of the Baath party. The Kiowas provided air cover while ground troops surrounded a hospital and searched it, but they didn't find Saddam. It was the first of many Saddam chases for Darkhorse troop. They called them "Elvis sightings."

JIM CORNELL—

Everybody in the military wanted to be the one to catch him. You get all excited about it and get out there as fast as you can and it turns out to be boring and nothing really happens. Still you get equally excited every time because you want to be the person that catches the number one bad guy.

Generally what we did on a mission like that is we would go out there, we would provide them security with a little heavier weapons than what they carried on the ground. If they did get into something, we could support them with rockets or whatever kind of fires we had available.

That was kind of an on-call type deal. Our primary mission was to make sure nobody approached, and do a little farther out reconnaissance. They are limited by what they can see from ground level. We would make sure that nobody was moving toward them and we would make sure that nobody got away from them from inside the perimeter without them seeing.

Kimberly ran the daily briefs for the troop, presenting the overall picture, and then turned it over to the team leaders in specialty areas. Donovan briefed in fuel and ammo. "Everybody briefed their own piece of the pie and Kimberly oversaw all of them," Donovan said. "She made sure all the pieces fit together right." Then Kimberly would add any information she got from higher ups and see if there were any unanswered questions. After the brief, it was Kimberly's responsibility to go to headquarters to fill in the missing pieces.

Kimberly had to make a lot of decisions on the spot and she stood by her decisions and stood up for her troops. "She never minded getting a butt chewing by superiors," Donovan said. "She never minded getting in trouble if she thought she was doing the right thing."

Kimberly never took it personally. Eric Pitkus, Kimberly's first sergeant, would be pretty upset after some of the more unpleasant encounters with their commander. "Then I'd walk out and see her with a smile on her face and I'd figure everything's good," Eric said.

Kimberly's meetings with Lieutenant Colonel Artman, the battalion commander, were generally low key. Kimberly reported to the battalion headquarters several times a week when key administrative staff and the five aviation unit commanders planned missions and discussed day-to-day administrative matters. She took meticulous notes and studied the paperwork through black frame glasses that the other officers teasingly called her "librarian glasses."

LEE CONLEY—
She wanted to be sure she had all the information to make the right decision for her soldiers. She was always going to the meetings. It could have been handed down to someone else, but she took a lot of the burden on herself."

Kimberly was equally focused at intelligence briefings before flights. Most pilots just wanted a quick update, but Kimberly wanted to know everything that had happened in the past few hours as well as what was happening right then. Capt. Crystal Armour Boring, one of the intelligence officers appreciated her attentiveness:

Every pilot had to come to the consolidated Intel section to get a briefing before they flew. A lot of times I would give an intel brief to pilots and a lot of times they were 'yeah, yeah, whatever,' and they would kind of blow you off and just wanted to get out there and fly. But with Kim, she would come in and she would sit down and she would lean forward and look at you because she wanted to hear exactly what you had to say.

She wanted to know everything. It was refreshing. She was so sincere and she would thank you—every time she would thank you for the briefing. She was really serious about hearing what you had to say. She would ask questions. She wanted to be aware of everything. She took her job so seriously.

She would come back in after a mission—we ask our pilots to do a debriefing, where they have to write down different things they saw. A lot of times the pilots would come back in and say they didn't see anything and that's all they would write. She would write long, detailed briefings about what she saw. There were details of time, everything and she had the neatest handwriting. Super neat. She would write down everything so you could print out the best intel for the next pilot going out there. As tired as she would be, she would still come back and write a full page or more about what she saw. She thought about the next person going out there. She would come back in and say I saw it at this time and at this location and she would have a grid of where it happened, so you could brief the next pilot and say the last pilot saw this at this location, so you want to be aware of this area here. She'd go up to the map and point it out to you. She was so dedicated. It was nice to see someone like that. And she would thank you. She would thank you after a briefing and then the door was only four feet away and she would turn around and thank me again and wink and smile. It made you feel good because it was a genuine gesture and you could tell she was being so sincere.

Kimberly became Crystal's role model, and two years after Kimberly's death, as Crystal prepared to take command, she reflected on Kimberly's example:

She was so intense but she was still a lady. She was an excellent leader. She was able to exert her authority without raising her voice, without being mean. She was still a lady. She was still beautiful, and she was a soldier. Despite her overwhelming responsibilities as a troop commander, she was still a lovely person, she was still a sweet person, she was still a humble person.

Crystal first encountered Kimberly over the telephone in Afghanistan. Crystal was in the task force intelligence office in Kandahar and periodically called the brigade headquarters at Bagram. One day Kimberly answered the phone.

"Wow, I didn't know there were any females there," Crystal said, happy to hear another woman's voice.

"I didn't know there were females there either," Kimberly replied.

They met briefly face to face back at Ft. Bragg, outside Lieutenant Colonel Bricker's office just before Kimberly went to Jump School. Kimberly recognized Crystal's name on her uniform.

"You're Captain Armour!" Kimberly exclaimed.

CRYSTAL ARMOUR BORING—

It was only a moment and she was called into Lieutenant Colonel Bricker's office. The next time I talked to her was in Iraq. She was always so quiet, and she was super friendly. It was like she was always deep in thought. Just watching her she was always so meticulous about everything she was doing. I would see her in the showers at night because she would be just getting back from her mission out flying and I was just getting off my night shift. She worked super long hours. She'd always speak to you and always smile and ask how you were doing.

You could just see it in her face that she loved what she was doing. She just wanted to be the best in what she was doing and that was evident in everything she did. She was super serious and super focused. She wanted to be the best in everything she was doing. It was awesome to watch. Yet she had no airs whatsoever.

Kimberly loved the flying and personally took on a lot of dangerous missions, Eric said. "She spread the wealth out, but she always made sure she or a platoon leader was out there to be the air mission commander."

As one of few women on the base, Kimberly "could never just blend in and disappear. There were always eyes on her," Mac said. That could make her job tougher at times. Kimberly withstood more testing than the average male, but always maintained a calm demeanor with her troops.

"She was a very private person when it came to talking about the seriousness of the mission," Mac said.

But Kimberly's troops could read her like a book. When they saw Kimberly eating more ice cream and drinking more Diet Cokes, they knew that things were getting tough.

Well, another month has come and gone here at TQ. The days are moving faster now that we have settled into a schedule. We have also endured our first Haboob, a giant sand storm that resembles nuclear winter. Darkhorse has launched many times as QRF (Quick Reaction Force) to support ground troops in our area of operation. Our missions also consist of a lot of reconnaissance work to help the ground units gather intelligence for future operations. The crew chiefs are doing a great job keeping the aircraft mission capable and supporting the high tempo of our missions.

TQ hosted its first talent show, "Iraqi Idol," last Sunday. SGT Michael Duncan serenaded the audience with his guitar and sang two songs. All of Darkhorse thought that he should have won and didn't have enough cash to bribe the judges into our way of thinking. The show was a big success and is now taking place every other week. We are also looking forward to Drew Carey coming to perform for us November 22.

The pilots took part in a mini-SERE course hosted by Air Force rescue specialists this week. In this one-day vacation to East Jabip, the other side of the airfield, we practiced our desert survival and evading skills with a short evasion lane. It also gave some of us good practice falling down sand dunes. It was valuable training and a good refresher course.

The new dining facility opens this coming week and we are very excited about the new food that the civilian contractors will be cooking. They will serve four meals a day, which will be great for us on the night shift. We have also been enjoying the fine cuisine offered by the Haji Mart, a restaurant run by locals. It's no Outback, but it does offer a break from the usual Mess Hall mystery meals. Oh yeah, they have ice cream, too!

—Kimberly's November 15, 2003 "Darkhorse News"
to families at home

November 21, 2003

Darkhorse had an aircraft accident this morning at about 0100. EVERYONE IS OKAY! The aircraft was completely destroyed, but the crew walked away with only scrapes, bumps and bruises. I was in one of the aircraft on the scene but it was not my aircraft that was involved. Based on the severity of the crash, no one should have survived. It is a miracle from God. Words cannot describe my emotions right now. The Troop is doing okay. . .many are very shaken up to say the least.

—e-mail Kimberly sent to Dale and me, and to Will

November 27, 2003

It's been a long time since I was home for Thanksgiving. Maybe next year. I slept through lunch today, but got up for midnight chow . . . it was okay. The weather has

been bad here so not much flying. That's okay. We needed a break. The guys from the
accident are doing fine. Everyone is doing fine, actually. We all have a lot to be thankful
for.   —Kimberly's Thanksgiving e-mail to us

There was a lot to be thankful for, as Kimberly wrote in a mid-December e-mail to Rick:

You may have heard—they shot down one of our 58Ds the other day. Crew escaped and was rescued quickly. The aircraft caught fire and was destroyed. My troop had a crash at the end of November and destroyed an aircraft. In total, our TF has lost 4 58Ds in 3 months—not a good average so far. Luckily, no major injuries and no loss of life.

Willy was in the November 21 crash along with CWO Robert Moody, one of Kimberly's pilots whom I'd met earlier during a visit to Ft. Bragg. Later, in an incident on December 9, Captain Robin Brown, the only other aviation brigade female company commander at Al Taqaddum was shot down in a Kiowa 58D.

Robin and her copilot managed to land, get away from the area of danger, and were rescued about an hour later. When Robin got back Kimberly hugged her, an unusual display of emotion that took Robin by surprise. Kimberly said she'd been close to tears, and that surprised Robin also, because Kimberly was usually all business. Even when they walked to the female shower tent together, they talked shop, discussing the challenges of being commanders and how to keep their troops focused on the mission instead of family back home. Joking about the smell of living in tents with a bunch of guys was as close as they had come before to personal conversation between two women. When Kimberly was shot down, Robin understood Kimberly's emotion. "I knew exactly how she felt," Robin said. "It was like a kick in the gut."

Kimberly made a quick call home that day, to let us know she was okay before we saw any news about the crash and became alarmed. She only had a moment to talk. She said she'd seen both pilots and had given them hugs, and they were okay. It was the last phone call we would receive from her. Later she e-mailed me with more details.

"I would have had to come home if those guys had died. . . . just couldn't handle it," Kimberly wrote in her e-mail to me after Willy and Rob crashed.

"Kimberly, I cannot even begin to imagine what you went through during/after the accident. The miracle that kept them alive is almost unbelievable. . . . Hopefully you will never be tested again, but you have the confidence to know that you can handle any situation immediately. Do not doubt yourself, baby . . . you've proved your mental and physical toughness over and over. Just believe in yourself," I wrote back.

Big news broke the routine of combat zone life a few days later, on December 13, 2003, when Saddam Hussain was captured in Tikrit by the army's 4th Infantry Division and Task Force 121 in an operation known as Red Dawn. The day stood out because it was a step forward, but everyone knew that nothing had really changed. "It didn't mean that was the end of the war," Robin said. "It was exciting, but we were still fighting the people we were fighting."

Kimberly echoed that sentiment in an Instant Message we received at home:

> It was a big day here today. We are all excited. Guess how we found out? By watching the news! You'd think we would get some inside scoop or something. Not the case. I am doing okay. We had today off and most of the guys played flag football. I took some pictures and just chilled out. We have some missions coming up—the recent news doesn't change much here.

Long before the holiday season arrived, Kimberly, Willy, and several others planned a surprise Christmas party for the troop. They enlisted help from the FRG (Family Readiness Group), us and other families back home, and packages started arriving that were secreted away. By Thanksgiving, gifts had started to arrive. I was glad to be a part of her plans and glad she was doing something special to celebrate, because Christmas had always been a special time for Kimberly. We got a Christmas tree and packaged up Santa hats for the soldiers and other goodies and sent them on.

I try to give all my friends and relatives something to make them happy. Giving gifts is the best thing about Christmas in my opinion.

—Kimberly Hampton, fourth grade Christmas book

Two days before Christmas, Kimberly and her coconspirators met in an empty tent that had been a temporary office and was no longer used. They put up some small Christmas trees that had been sent by the families. They wound garland and lights around the trees and the inside of the tent. The gifts that had been hidden away were unpacked and stacked around the trees. Some were wrapped in fancy store-bought paper and others were wrapped in art paper hand decorated by a second grade class taught by Willy's sister's mother-in-law in a small Texas community.

"There were packages everywhere and they were having a great time getting everything ready for the party," said Joel, who popped in while he was at that end of the base to wish everyone a Merry Christmas.

Dec. 24, 2003
Merry Christmas Eve!
Dear Mom and Dad,
Merry Christmas! I'm writing this on Christmas Eve, though I probably won't get to send it out to you until Christmas Day. I am going to try to call on Christmas night here, Christmas morning there. . . .

Tonight we had the TF Wolfpack Christmas party. It was pretty fun. They brought the commanders on stage and embarrassed us a little bit—it made the soldiers laugh so I guess that's all that matters. I handed out the Santa hats to the guys. They love them! We're going to get a picture tomorrow after we all have lunch together at the DFAC [dining facility]. Tomorrow night we are having the Troop Christmas party and we will hand out presents. We do the White Elephant game like we did in Korea. . . .

Wish I could be there to celebrate with you guys. I am with you in spirit, always. I love you. Merry Christmas.
Kimberly

On Christmas Day, everyone wore the Santa hats we had sent and gathered in the mess hall for a traditional holiday meal with turkey, ham, mashed potatoes, and all the trimmings like at home. Kimberly gave everyone in her troop a pair of flannel pajama bottoms Willy's family and friends had sent and told them to wear them to the empty office tent for a pajama party later that night when the pilots who had to fly that day returned.

Everyone gathered in the decorated tent, wearing the pajamas. Some of the soldiers wore the Santa hats and others wore their Cavalry Stetsons. They snacked on little sausages, cheese, and chips. The presents flowed. The second graders sent soap, laundry detergent, and other necessities that were hard to get in Iraq. An elk rancher, whom Willy's mother worked for in Texas, outfitted a gift box for everyone in the troop with a thermos, hot chocolate, flannel throw blankets, flashlights and more. There were more gifts from us and other families as well. Kimberly had contacted her troops' families at home and arranged for them to send Christmas presents addressed to her, so that everyone also got presents from their own family at home.

For the White Elephant game, everyone put his or her name in a hat and the names were drawn one by one. There were gifts for everyone, but many of them exchanged hands a few times before the night was over.

DONOVAN McCARTNEY—

The first guy would pick a present. They were all wrapped so you didn't know what they were. Everybody after him, if you unwrapped your present and didn't like it, you could trade with someone before you. It was a lot of fun. You'd get something you really liked and someone after you would grab it from you and you'd get another. It was the first time I'd ever done something like that.

We had the Christmas tree with the lights and decorations. Her parents or somebody mailed her the tree. The box came to her. Every couple of days, we'd get packages, and everybody looked forward to mail day. She was always getting packages, and it was a curiosity to us. It turned out that her parents were stocking her up with stuff for Christmas, not only for her but for her to give to everybody else. One day she got this huge package that was about six feet tall and about two or three feet wide. It turned out to be a Christmas tree. She didn't tell us until Christmas Day

For a short time they were removed from the constant stress of the war zone and it felt like Christmas.

ADAM CAMARANO—

I still had to fly missions that day. I'd never known Christmas without my family, my mom and dad and my sister and the dog. She went out of her way to make it less emotional being away from the families. We had as good a Christmas party as you could have had considering the conditions.

Everybody had a great time. Especially Kimberly.

Will flew in from Baghdad on December 28. It was the second time he and Kimberly were together since she left Ft. Bragg for Iraq. His first visit to Al Taqaddum, a few days before Christmas, was short. He and Kimberly had dinner together but he couldn't stay long. This time they had about three or four hours together. He gave her a watch he'd bought for her, they went to dinner, and spent the evening talking:

We had dinner and just hung out. We just walked around and talked. We went back to her company area, and met some of the guys I'd met before and talked to them a little bit and then we went and got ice cream. There was a little market that had a couple stores on the airfield, stores run by locals who were selling knick-knacks from Iraq and rugs, and they had a little snack bar area where they had a little ice cream shop. Apparently Kimberly was on good terms with the ice cream guys. When she walked in with me their eyes lit up and they knew exactly what she wanted. Vanilla ice cream and lime sherbet, and they gave her two extra scoops they wouldn't give me for the same price.

We sat down and talked for about an hour there. It was the first time in a long time that we talked about our future, and us, and how things were going. I know I was leaving to go home, at least just temporarily in February, and she was thinking at that point that she may be home in April or May. We started talking about what we wanted to do when we got home. We talked about taking a trip to a beach somewhere, maybe down to the Caribbean.

Kimberly was not sure before going over there whether or not she was going to stay in the army or if she was going to get out. She was kind of torn. She really wanted to stay in the military. She liked the job, but she had definitely thought about two other options. She thought about going to law school. There was a way she could do that through the army, and she would have stayed in the army as a lawyer. Before leaving for Iraq she took the [LSAT] tests, but because of her quick departure that didn't pan out. She rushed through the process and didn't finish it up before heading overseas. And then she thought about getting out and doing something else totally different and being a mother. She wasn't set at that point on being in the military for a full career, which had been her goal a few years prior. She was starting to change her mind a little. I think her career was starting to conflict with some of the things she wanted to do later on. She was really enjoying being a commander and being over there, but she had some big decisions to make when she got home.

She wanted a family. I don't think it was anything we were going to start immediately after getting married, but within a year or two. We talked and hinted about it in e-mails. Kimberly, in Korea, was always involved with orphanages that our unit sponsored. She was always sponsoring kids for Thanksgiving dinner, bringing kids over for Christmas, as always going out of her way to take part in those activities. You could tell just by the way she interacted with the kids. It was definitely something that she wanted of her own when the time came.

I couldn't see her just staying home. She'd want to do something. She thought about using her tennis, either teaching or coaching tennis. I think that's probably what she would have ended up doing if she decided to get out of the army. Maybe coach at the high school level at first and work her way up. I think that probably would have brought her the most joy professionally if she wasn't going to stay in the army.

She also could have stayed in the military twenty years and been very happy doing that. She had thought about finishing as a troop commander and then going out and being an instructor at the National Training Center in California. That would give her the opportunity to still fly, be connected with the action side of the army, but also be there in an instructor role. She wanted to be either teaching or instructing people.

Before Will had to return to Baghdad, Kimberly told him about her upcoming mission a few days away. The ground forces were going into Fallujah itself, and they would be flying in the daytime over some pretty contested areas, she said. It would be their most dangerous mission so far, she told him:

> It wasn't going to be an easy day, but she wanted to be there. If something bad happened, she wanted be sure she could do her job and keep people safe.

Will was on night duty the evening before the big mission and called her about seven, but they only got to talk about ten minutes:

> I got bombarded with work to do on my end, so I said, "I'll call you back in a couple hours before you turn in for the night because I want to talk to you before your mission tomorrow." We got off the phone and then she called me back around ten o'clock, and I had just left to go do something. I got back and had a message: Hey, Captain Hampton called you and she's only going to be there a few more minutes. So I tried to call her back, and she had just left by the time I called her, so we played phone tag.
>
> She had sent me an e-mail before she left:
> "This mission is going to be the most dangerous one we've been on and I can't wait to tell you about it when it's over."

Before she went to sleep, Kimberly set the alarm on the new watch Will had given her. The alarm was set for 5:02 AM.

An OH-58D Kiowa Warrior helicopter from 2nd Squadron, 17th Cavalry Regiment swoops by a Humvee from 1st Battalion, 327th Infantry Regiment during a weapons cache search near Kirkuk, Iraq. *Journalist 1st Class Jeremy L. Wood (USN), defenseimagery.mil*

Two OH-58D Kiowa Warrior helicopters fly a close air support mission.
Master Sergeant Scott Wagers (USAF), defenseimagery.mil

A row of OH-58D Kiowa helicopters from 2nd Squadron, 17th Cavalry Regiment sit mission ready
on the flight line at Forward Operating Base Warrior, Iraq, June 24, 2006.
Journalist 1st Class Jeremy L. Wood (USN), defenseimagery.mil

CHAPTER 11

BIRD DOWN: JANUARY 2, 2004

I t was a cold morning, just above freezing and the sun was just coming up when Mac, whose tent was near Kimberly's, heard her coughing outside. She was getting over a cold but couldn't shake the persistent cough. Mac had worked night shift and had just turned off his light to go to sleep when he heard Kimberly's dry hacking cough. He knew Kimberly was flying on the mission and thought about going out and saying hi or even having breakfast, but he didn't and regretted that decision later.

Kimberly and Donovan were about to get in their helicopter when one of the guys who wasn't flying that day came up and snapped their picture. About five minutes later they took off.

They flew in teams of two helicopters. Because of the seriousness of the mission the battalion commander, Lieutenant Colonel Artman, was flying that day with Lee in the lead helicopter on Kimberly and Donovan's team. Kimberly was the team leader and the air mission commander. The Kiowas made passes over the weapons market as the ground guys went in, creating a noisy deterrent, ready to give backup fire support if needed, and looking for weapons dealers trying to flee the market on flatbed trucks, called bongos, filled with weapons.

LEE CONLEY—
We give the commander on the ground an extra set of eyes. You can see behind

the building he can't see behind, so you can do a lot for him. We could fly over the rooftops really fast and look for potential hazards to them. It was pretty crowded in the market, a lot of civilians, a lot of soldiers running around. It was pretty chaotic down there for awhile. Flying over the buildings and looking at the rooftops, we are looking at the rooftops and we are looking at the alleyways and things of that nature, too.

After a little over an hour of flying, Kimberly's team gave a battle handover to the second team, briefing them over the radio and landed at the FARP (forward army refueling point) to refuel. While she was back on the ground, Kimberly caught a ride with one of the ground soldiers to the bathrooms. She also had a moment to visit with Joel Campbell from Clinton, and they chatted about home until it was time to head out again.

Willy was on second team, flying with Andy Reiter, a friend of Kimberly's from flight school. He worked at the battalion office directly for Lieutenant Colonel Artman and was on the mission with him. Adam and Henry Quiles flew in the second helicopter on Willy and Andy's team. Activity had started picking up around the marketplace and the American ground troops were hauling out weapons by the truckload. They called for more trucks, bread trucks and anything else they could get, to haul the weapons out, Willy said. The mission was going well.

Ground troops had seen a couple of Iraqis on rooftops and Willy's team did some rooftop checks just before giving battle handover back to Kimberly's team. They circled southwest of the city and saw some Iraqis on the ground indicating that there was something going on in the area. Willy's group passed the information on to Kimberly's team and returned to the FARP.

Kimberly's team flew for another hour or so and was getting close to the point in fuel where they needed to head back. Lee was on the radio trying to contact Willy's team for a handover, but couldn't get them and figured they might still be in the fuel area, where radios are kept off. He radioed to Kimberly and told her they probably had enough fuel for another pass. Kimberly was talking on the radio with the ground commanders and didn't hear what Lee had said.

They were flying over some farm fields a couple of miles south of Fallujah. Lee was flying low, about thirty to fifty feet off the ground in the lead aircraft. Kimberly called back and asked what he had said. He told her again there was enough gas to do another pass or two.

"Roger that. Let's go," Kimberly said in a relaxed tone of voice.

Lee turned his aircraft to the right and headed northeast toward Fallujah. He radioed back to Kimberly and Donovan what he was going to do on the inbound, instructions that typically don't need a response:

> I told her I was going to cross the river at a certain point, hop over the bridge and then hit the objective going south to north. About the time I hit the river, I heard the ground guys start screaming on the radio.
>
> All they were saying was bird down, bird down, bird down. I laid the aircraft over as hard as I could. I got down to the river valley. I thought, okay, one, they're shooting at me, or two, they're shooting at them. Either way, we're getting shot at. I didn't know who it was. So I broke hard left back to the west, still alongside of the river. I'm calling on the radio to try to get contact with them. I'm calling "Darkhorse Six" . . . "Darkhorse Six." I turn around. I don't see anything where I think they should have been. So I do a little figure eight pattern to try to get back to where I thought they might have been. I turned left, turned to the west, did kind of a circle and headed back in the direction we came from. I didn't see anything, so I came back to the west. I can't find them, I don't know what happened to them, and I don't know if the shooter is still there trying to get me also. My main concern is to find the aircraft, and if they did go down, get help to them. My other concern is to make sure we don't become a second aircraft down, compounding the problem for them.
>
> I can't get hold of them so I switch my radio to the ground guys.
>
> "Where did you see it? What's your location?"
>
> "South of us."
>
> "Okay, where are you?"
>
> I flew back around to the west looking for smoke and saw a pile of smoke I thought might have been a burned aircraft, so I fly to that. It's just smoke from someone burning grass in a field. Going to that, I turned to the left and I looked down and I saw something

that looked unnatural in a field, so I brought it back around hard right, and I saw the tail boom of the aircraft.

"I found pieces of the aircraft."

"We're rolling! We're rolling south."

I'm talking to the ground guys and trying to get contact with Adam Camarano's team, to get them to launch out, because now I'm out there alone, single ship, and before all of this started, we were already at the bottom of our fuel. Now I'm getting past the critical point. I can't remember who I got a hold of, if it was Willy or if it was Camarano.

"We've got an aircraft down."

The tail boom of the aircraft was actually across a street from where the aircraft actually impacted, but the spot where the aircraft impacted was hard to see unless you were right above it or saw it at the right angle of where it went into the concrete wall, because it was in a grove of thirty or forty-foot-tall palms.

I started doing some more searches, talking to the ground guys. They're coming south. They're saying they don't see the aircraft. They think it went into the water. I started heading back over to the water to see if I can see where it had gone in, and as I was doing that, I see parts of the rotor system sticking out just behind the concrete wall. The main rotor hub didn't have any blades on it. It was pretty messed up. I went there, saw the fuselage of the aircraft. I didn't see Kimberly or Donovan. I just saw the main fuselage of the aircraft in the palm grove. The ground guys are about two hundred meters up the road. So I go into a tight circle and I start screaming into the radio to those guys.

"They're underneath me! They're underneath me!"

I didn't see any movement down there. I now shift to the mode of getting that other team out, and getting the ground guys to them to give them first aid and to cover the ground guys because the shooter's around there somewhere.

I'm covering the ground guys as they come in. They get to the wall and they start digging through the wreckage and they throw out a purple smoke grenade to mark the spot. The other team shows up and I give them a quick battle handover.

I'm very low on gas at this point. Lieutenant Colonel Artman and I go back and we landed in the refuel. We get gas, do some coordination with the brigade headquarters. They kept asking us status of the crew.

"Unknown."

The pilots on the second team knew it was almost time for Kimberly's team to come back in for refueling and decided to go ahead and get airborne, even though Kimberly's team hadn't called for them yet. They were taking off to the north toward Fallujah and planning to circle and be in the air and ready when "everything started going wrong and we heard all the radio chatter," Willy said.

An aircraft was down.

"That is a horrible, horrible very sick feeling you get when you hear something like that," Andy said. The two helicopters flew toward Fallujah as fast as possible monitoring the radio for more information.

When Willy and Andy, who were in the lead helicopter, heard a voice on the radio say southwest of Fallujah, they remembered the group of Iraqis they had seen on the ground. They knew the area was a hotspot because other aircraft had been hit there recently, including a Chinook that went down carrying soldiers headed to R&R about a month earlier.

"We couldn't see anything from the distance but we knew where to go," Andy said. They flew toward the purple smoke spiraling skyward and spotted the downed helicopter in the corner of the palm grove a kilometer or two from the surrounded Fallujah marketplace. The helicopter had hit the high wall surrounding the grove of trees and had rolled over on top of the wall before coming to rest. They provided cover as a ground crew rammed a vehicle into the mud and brick wall and knocked it down to get to the downed Kiowa quickly. Andy and Willy watched from above as Kimberly and Donovan were pulled from the wreckage. They tried to get information on the radio about their condition, but they knew the answers wouldn't be good.

Word came over the radio that Kimberly had been killed and Donovan was unconscious. Adam, who was team leader, had to relay the news back to headquarters at the base. A few minutes later ground crews relayed the news that Donovan had regained consciousness, and it looked like he would be all right.

The pilots had to cover the crash scene and direct ground crews, continue to provide security and reconnaissance for the ground operations on Fallujah and try to locate the person who had shot Kimberly and Donovan down. The air force sent jets in to assist.

"It got busy really fast for me," said Adam, who had to coordinate operations between the Kiowas and the jets. He'd never personally known anyone killed in action before. As commander, Kimberly was a parent figure for her soldiers. She was like their mother. Adam had been assigned to the Darkhorse Troop only two weeks before deployment to Iraq and had been unsure about working for a woman. It was a busy time, but Kimberly had made the time to help him sort out his new responsibilities as a platoon leader and set him up for success. She quickly proved to him that she was more than capable and that women can serve in the army as effectively as men. She was firm and fair. No one could push her around. She was one of his role models. Adam forced himself to think about the mission at hand and not the helicopter on the ground.

"It would start to creep into my mind then I would kind of get behind in what I was trying to do," Adam said. "I had to force myself to concentrate on what was going on and what I needed to do. There wasn't anything more I could do for her at that point in time."

Actually, there was one more thing. After Donovan and Kimberly were loaded into vehicles, the two Kiowas flew overhead and escorted the group of five or six Humvees to a hospital at an infantry base just outside of Fallujah to make sure they didn't run into any problems during the ten to fifteen minute drive.

Jen and Jim were back at the base listening to the radio traffic. They had been scheduled to fly that day, but Kimberly had changed the scheduled rotation and put her own team on the mission and assigned Jen and Jim's team as the quick reaction force. That meant waiting in the tactical operations center and listening to the radio in case something happened and responding only if needed. Jen and Jim were both disappointed to miss the big mission, and Jim had questioned Kimberly about her decision.

It boiled down to the team mixes, crew mixes and risk assessment, Jim said. "It was the best overall balance across the board. She had to look at the big picture and balance it across the board as best she could."

Jen and Jim, both experienced pilots, were teamed with one of the most junior pilots and a task force safety officer who was filling in. The four had never flown together as a team and couldn't go to the rehearsal for the mission because they'd had quick reaction force duty that day, too, and were tied to the desk.

"It was higher risk to send out a team that collectively didn't work together much," Jim said. They'd also missed getting a lot of details about the mission in the rehearsal. "A commander's responsibility is to assess the risk."

Jen was in the TOC when she heard a man's voice on the radio say he thought an aircraft went down. She listened impatiently to a confusion of voices sorting out whether a helicopter really was down and the status of the pilots. Once it was clear an aircraft was indeed down, she called Jim.

"Can you come up here for a minute?" Jen asked.

Her tone struck Jim as odd.

As he walked into the room, he heard on the radio that Darkhorse Six was down. They decided to get ready to respond. They grabbed the safety officer and other pilot and rushed to their aircraft. They were ready to go, but a senior officer put them on hold.

Jim was furious.

"I finally talked them into letting us move out of parking and be prepositioned to take off and that's when we heard the call," Jim said.

They sat in the helicopter, ready to assist and waiting for permission when a voice on the radio said Darkhorse Six was dead.

Jen looked at Jim in disbelief.

"Stay focused" Jim said. "Focus on the mission."

Jen had been the air mission commander the last time an aircraft went down, and Jim was concerned about her. But she pushed her emotions aside and focused on the mission.

Time after time Jen had practiced for this day in training drills. "It is driven into your mind from very early on to know the chain of command and to take charge if your leader gets killed," Jen said, reflecting back on that day several years later. For the rest of the mission on that terrible day, she forced herself "to believe this was just an exercise" and that Kimberly "would be there to critique our performance when we landed."

Once in the air, Jen and Jim could see parts of the aircraft on the ground, but Kimberly already had been taken away and Adam's team had just finished escorting the ambulance back to the base.

Jim and Jen knew what had just happened but had no details about how it happened. They tried to keep moving as they provided security for the ground crews because they knew the enemy was still out there. There were a few sporadic fire fights, but the marketplace mission had pretty much calmed down and was wrapping up. The infantry was securing the crash site and chasing the suspected shooter through some houses on that side of the river. They were looking for a particular type and color of vehicle the suspected shooter might be in, but it was one of the common vehicles driven by Iraqis, and they were everywhere. By the time the next troop came on duty and Jen and Jim returned to the base, things had pretty much died down and they were essentially providing security for the infantry securing the crash scene until they could recover the helicopter.

Once on the ground, Jen allowed the reality of Kimberly's death to sink in. This wasn't just an exercise and Kimberly "was not there when we landed," Jen said. In the days and weeks that followed Jen "had to fight the urge to believe that any second she would walk in ready to talk about what we did well and what we could improve on."

First Sergeant Eric Pitkus was sitting on an enlisted promotion board in an old Iraqi building that served as the battalion headquarters when he heard over the radio that an aircraft was down.

"A guy got on the radio and asked what the situation was with the pilots. Two or three minutes later you could hear the call that nobody wanted to hear," Eric said.

They stopped the board and shut down all communications from Iraq back to the States, which is normal procedure to prevent anyone from calling home until the family members were notified through proper channels. The battalion command sergeant major pulled Eric outside to discuss proper notification of the troops.

"Going in and telling your troop that their commander had died was a hard thing to do," Eric said. "The next two aircraft we sent up knew what had happened but nobody else knew." Eric stayed at the battalion headquarters until they had confirmation and then he had to tell the others in the troop. "It's kind of hard to lose somebody you work hand in hand with and then go down and with no emotion tell them what happened. I had a hard time with it. When I told the rest of the guys, some were upset, some pissed, plain out mad. Some guys took it pretty good. Some just had some issues with it," Eric said.

After Jen and Jim got back, the troop got together to figure out what to do. Everyone was sitting in shock staring at each other. It was quiet. Jen was now the senior officer in the troop.

"I guess the most appropriate thing to say now is 'you're released to manage your own time,'" Jen said, echoing the words Kimberly had used to dismiss her soldiers ever since Kuwait.

Everybody stayed there together for awhile. Most of them had been together for at least a year and they were a tight group. After a while people started drifting off alone or in pairs to deal with the shock in their own ways.

Adam had seen people killed before, but no one he knew personally:

It's not as personal as when it's somebody you know and it's your leader. It just made it extremely difficult because you didn't have that one person to look to, to say, "everything's going to be all right," because she was that person.

A few hours after Eric broke the news to the troop, he was notified that as Kimberly's first sergeant and someone who had worked closely with her, he would escort her home. He only had a few minutes to gather what he needed for the trip and board a Black Hawk helicopter that was already running, waiting to fly him to Baghdad.

Kimberly's body was in a metal transport case with an American flag draped over it. He escorted her from Baghdad to Kuwait, and then flew in the belly of a Fed Ex plane to Dover Air Force base in Delaware. They landed around midnight, but despite the late hour, a small ceremony was held when Kimberly's body was moved from the plane and back on American soil. A general said a few words and a chaplain prayed.

ERIC PITKUS—
Every time they bring a body home from war, a general always comes out to the aircraft and the mortuary affairs personnel come out and they bring an army chaplain. They do a really nice ceremony right there. I was fighting off tears. It's a great respect that they present to the departed, but it's definitely something you don't want to do again.

Eric was supposed to escort Kimberly all the way home to Easley, but plans changed and others took over and he was sent right back to Iraq. The next morning he was on a C-17 heading back to Iraq. He missed Kimberly's memorial in Iraq and the funeral in Easley, but she wasn't alone when she came home to the country she'd given her life for. He was there with her.

ERIC PITKUS—

The energy that she put off, you couldn't work for somebody better. She loved doing what she was doing. All she wanted to be was a troop commander and she was able to do that.

Will was working nights and sleeping days, but after he couldn't get Kimberly back on the phone the night before the mission she was on his mind. He didn't sleep long before he woke up wondering how the mission was going and he couldn't get back to sleep. He got up about noon and walked over to the operations center, where CNN and FOX news were usually on. The ticker tape crawl at the bottom of the screen said a helicopter had been shot down and one person was dead and one was wounded. Will was sick with worry. A friend told him to just call over there and ask what he needed to know but Will couldn't make the call. He was afraid of what the voice on the other end of the line might say. His friends told him to get out of the operations center and try to relax. Will walked outside, pacing nervously. He went and found the chaplain. They said a prayer for Kimberly, and Will returned to the operations center.

A friend who knew the head guy handling casualties at the 82nd made the phone call for him. Will was too nervous to stay. He walked outside and talked with his commander. When he came back in, he saw "CPT Hampton" written on a piece of paper and knew. Unable to contain his emotions he went to his tent and started throwing things, startling some people who didn't know what had happened until his friend, the commander and the chaplain arrived to calm him down. They made arrangements to get him on the next plane back to the States to be with us in Easley.

Will was grateful. It was a unique and meaningful act of compassion for them to let him go, because he and Kimberly weren't yet married. They couldn't let him call us until we were properly notified, following military rules. The twelve hours until we were notified and Will could talk to us had been torture for him. Dale e-mailed Will three times begging for any information as the news was reported at home—a helicopter down—a Kiowa—a death.

"It hurt not to be able to talk to them," Will said. When he finally was allowed to call, "they were crushed and in shock. It just didn't seem real yet," Will said. Two hours later Will was on a C-17 cargo airplane on his way to South Carolina.

Donovan McCartney was in the hospital for a couple of days, but was back in time for Kimberly's memorial service at Al Taquaddum on January 6.

A stage was made from trailers. Kimberly's boots, weapon, helmet, and dog tags were displayed in front of a picture of her. Roll call was taken. Soldiers responded when their names were called. Kimberly's name was called.

"Captain Kimberly Hampton."

There was silence.

Andy Reiter, in his role as battalion adjutant, led the service and introduced the speakers. He read a list of milestones of Kimberly's military career: her commissioning as a second lieutenant, graduation from the Kiowa Warrior Advanced Qualification Course, her participation in Operation Enduring Freedom in Afghanistan and more.

"We gather here to celebrate the life of a hero. The most eloquent of words are inadequate to express our sorrow," said Lieutenant Colonel Artman, the first of several speakers. "She commanded with moral conviction, steel in her backbone, and earned her soldiers' respect through her actions."

Jen Leidel read the 23rd Psalm, moving from the lectern as she uttered the last word, wanting more than anything for the entire nightmare to be over.

"Captain Hampton always led from the front, always encouraged us to do the right thing. She was always available to us to help us understand a situation or guide us through a difficult time," said Spec. Ruben Olyano.

"She was like a breath of fresh air, mixing old traditions with the dawn of a new age coming," said CWO Rick Olivarez. "She never missed an opportunity to let the soldiers know how much she appreciated them, always ending with that warm smile and subtle wink.

"I have no doubt that as you are greeted in heaven, the Lord Almighty is now enjoying your warm smile and subtle wink," Oliveraz said.

As the other female commander in the unit, Capt. Robin Brown was asked to speak. She had been eating lunch and getting ready to go on duty when someone came into the chow hall and said, "Captain Hampton's bird went down," and somehow she knew it was bad. She raced to a radio and when she heard "one female KIA," she knew the worst. The circumstances paralleled her crash but the outcome was so tragically different. Kimberly was shot down about two kilometers from where Robin's aircraft had gone down. It was about the same time of day and Robin also had been in the tail helicopter. All she could think was "why was it her. Why wasn't it me?"

Kimberly "wasn't about pomp and circumstance and would be embarrassed at the magnitude of this memorial, however she most deserves it," Robin said when she spoke at the memorial. She carried the speech in her notebook for a long time afterward because she didn't want to forget. It was a reminder that she survived for a reason and not to ever take life for granted again.

Photo collage made by Kimberly's troops at her memorial service in Iraq.

A Bible passage Chaplain (Capt.) Joseph Kilonzo read toward the end of the service, well known verses from Ecclesiastes, addressed the thoughts that whirled in Robin's mind: "To every thing there is a season, a time for every purpose under heaven. . . . a time to be born, a time to die."

The chaplain spoke of how Kimberly "carried herself with dignity and could light up a room by simply walking in the door." She remains "airborne with us in spirit and she must never be forgotten."

The honor guard fired a salute and four Kiowa Warriors flew overhead in the fallen aviator formation.

"The aircraft breaking formation represents the loss to our ranks," Andy explained from the lectern, and invited those gathered to come forward to pay their respects. As the first members of Darkhorse Troop reached Kimberly's picture, helmet, and boots displayed on the stage, they lingered, until they all were there together, and with arms around each other, bade her farewell in an impromptu and emotional gesture.

"It was tough sitting there in the audience listening to all these people talking about her and knowing she was never going to come back," said Donovan, who brought his tattered copy of the program home from Iraq

Missing man formation flown at memorial service held for Kimberly in Iraq.

with him, along with the picture taken of him and Kimberly just before they took off on her final mission.

The memorial service was moving, but fell short of the mark for cavalry members, who weren't allowed to wear their Stetsons to the service.

"Can't they have the cavalry hat?" Lieutenant Colonel Viola, who had presided over Kimberly's change of command at Ft. Bragg six months earlier, had asked at the rehearsal the day before the service. He was the Black Hawk battalion commander, but he also was cavalry and knew how important the Stetson was to Kimberly and her troop. He'd tried to make his point, but the cavalry hat "was definitely nonnegotiable," he said.

Willy figured that because the service was going to be videotaped, the decision makers wanted uniformity and didn't want them to stand out in their Stetsons. But the Stetsons are a meaningful symbol for cavalry troopers who felt that Kimberly certainly would have agreed. So they planned a private memorial service the next night.

Kimberly's Stetson was displayed instead of her helmet and her spurs were on her boots at the cavalry memorial. Willy prepared a PowerPoint video. He gathered every photo he could locate from anyone who had digital pictures and put music behind it. Then someone read the results of the mission. An astronomical number of weapons were captured. Based on later intelligence briefs, they later learned some local big guys were captured, as well.

Then there was an open forum for anyone who wanted to speak. People stood up at random and told stories. It got pretty emotional and tears started to flow. Almost everyone present was cavalry, but there were a few exceptions. Jen spotted Lt. Col. Jim Viola and his command sergeant major and wondered why they were there, because they were with the Black Hawk battalion and not part of the cavalry troops. She was surprised when Lieutenant Colonel Viola stood up to speak, but she never got to hear what he had to say. Before he could begin, someone came in and stopped the service.

"Is this a joke?" Jen wondered.

Lieutenant Colonel Viola wasn't sure what was happening either.

"I thought they were trying to bust up the memorial. I couldn't believe it," he said.

Viola wanted to address the small cavalry memorial gathering to express his pride in having had the opportunity to know Kimberly and to have passed her the Darkhorse troop guidon at her change of command. He'd been on a mission near where Kimberly was shot down on January 2 when he heard on the radio that an aircraft was down. He noted the time in his journal. It was 12:20 PM.

"Hello! Evening, Sir!" He still could hear Kimberly's voice in his mind. He missed her cheerful greeting and demeanor, her smile and her focus. "No matter how dirty or grimy she was, she looked like a librarian," he said. "I never saw her mad."

But as soon as he got up on stage and started to talk, an officer came in yelling. The camp had been attacked by rockets. The chapel where the service was held was at least a mile from the mortar attack, so they didn't hear it. Everyone was ordered to return to their assigned areas so everyone could be accounted for. The interrupted memorial service was never completed.

Lieutenant Colonel Viola and his sergeant major reported back to headquarters and learned the mortar had landed in the small room they shared in a long, low building where some of the top officers lived in five side-by-side rooms. The mortar had landed at the foot of Lieutenant Colonel Viola's cot.

The room was a shambles. The sergeant major's new air mattress was blown to pieces about the room. Their belongings were scattered and shredded.

They usually went to their room after dinner. Instead they had gone to Kimberly's cavalry memorial. It likely saved their lives. Command Sergeant Major Francisco Torres almost didn't go.

While they were at dinner, Viola told Torres he was going to the cavalry memorial and invited him to come along, but the sergeant major declined. He had already attended the ceremony for the whole brigade. After they finished eating, Viola headed toward the chapel and Torres headed in the opposite direction toward their room. He was about halfway to the room when something stopped him:

> Normally I go where the colonel goes, that's just protocol, but I felt strongly about not going to this because they were not my soldiers. I just didn't feel right about it. Then something overwhelmingly said

go to the chapel and say farewell to a fallen comrade. That's the least that you can do for this troop commander. She was more than competent. She was an excellent troop commander. I felt I had to go there. Something told me to go to the chapel. Thank God I went to the chapel. Thank Captain Hampton. I think she saved a lot of people.

As Viola and Torres talked about what had happened they cleaned their room. Both felt Kimberly had been watching over them.

About five other mortar rounds fell into the tent city area that night, but no one was killed or injured. As Jim and some of the others walked back to their tent, they heard some commotion in a Black Hawk troop tent nearby and stopped to investigate. A mortar round had come in through the roof of the tent. Two men had been inside when it hit. Everyone was stunned at what had happened. The round had bounced out of the tent without exploding.

CHAPTER 12

EASLEY, SOUTH CAROLINA:
JANUARY 2, 2004

I woke up about eight that Friday morning and logged onto AOL to check my e-mail, and saw that a helicopter had crashed in Iraq. I turned the TV on and then called Ft. Bragg, and was told no further information was available. Dale was already downstairs. After I called Ft. Bragg, I went down and told him there had been a crash. He told me later that I had a look in my eyes he'd never seen before. Maybe it was mother's intuition.

I felt an urgent need to be dressed and ready to travel. All I could think was that Kimberly could be injured. If that was the case, I wanted to be on the first plane to the army hospital in Germany.

"Please God," I prayed aloud in the shower, "don't let it be her."

The minutes ticked by excruciatingly slowly as the news trickled in. The picture grew grimmer with every tidbit of information. It happened near Fallujah. It was a Kiowa. Someone had died.

Leo Lesch had come down from Ft. Bragg to watch the New Year's Day football with Dale. Leo was so much like a brother to Kimberly that we considered him another son, like Sam. The three of us watched the news and waited for information. As more details were reported on the news, it became obvious that Kimberly's troop was probably involved, if not Kimberly herself.

"Kimberly! Please call!"

I begged the phone to ring.

Kimberly had called on December 9, less than a month earlier, when Robin Brown had been shot down. She'd called to say, "I don't know if you heard, but we're okay." She told us both pilots were fine and she'd given them both hugs. It was our last telephone conversation.

Please, telephone, ring!

"If it was someone in Kimberly's troop, she'll have her hands full," Leo said. "There would be no way she could call."

We knew that when a soldier is killed, communications are shut down until the family is notified by proper military authorities. I tried to cling to hope, but it was hard. I spent most of the day perched on the staircase near the front door with the phone beside me, staring out the window at the street, watching for the car I knew was coming.

Oh God, let them get here. Let this waiting end.

Dale e-mailed Will. There was no reply. Dale e-mailed him several more times during the day hoping for some shred of news.

In Iraq, Will read the e-mails and was sick that he couldn't reply and tell Dale and Ann what he already knew. Military protocol prevented any response until the family was properly notified.

I called Ft. Bragg several times and kept asking who the victim was. I finally learned it was someone in the battalion. No other information could be released.

I called Sarita Hinkie, Kimberly's childhood friend Sam's mother. We had stayed close over the years although they were in Oklahoma. Sarita had a brother who might have some connections. Maybe he could find something out. As we talked on the phone I kept my ear peeled for the call waiting beep in hopes that someone would call with news.

We peppered poor Leo with questions. Why hasn't Kimberly—or someone—called?

"Does the army have your new address?" Leo asked. We had recently moved to a new house just south of Easley. Kimberly had seen the new house before she left, but we hadn't moved in yet and it was empty when she visited.

"Have you gotten a pool table and mounted the dart board in the bonus room yet? Oh wait, I guess you didn't plan to do that, did you?" Kimberly had teased in an e-mail. "I think you should though. Would be fun!"

Leo's speculation was absolutely correct. The change of address paperwork hadn't gone through. I changed it with Ft. Bragg, but Kimberly hadn't signed the form to authorize the change because she was in Iraq. While we waited, worried, and prayed, an army warrant officer and a chaplain knocked on the door of our old house. We'd sold the house to a man who worked with Dale at Fort Hill Natural Gas. The man's wife answered the door and told the officers we'd moved. She called her husband at work and he went to Mike Haggard, the company operations manager.

Mike knew about the helicopter crash and our concern. Dale and Leo had been to the office earlier in the day, and talked to him there. We'd been friends with Mike for close to twenty years, even before Mike moved to Easley to work at Fort Hill. His daughter, Kathryn Grace, was about eight when they moved here, and Kimberly, who was in high school, nicknamed her "Squirt," and took the younger girl under her wing. Kimberly got Kathryn Grace interested in tennis, and now she was enjoying a successful high school tennis career in Kimberly's footsteps. The girls had remained close, and Kimberly had a framed picture Kathryn Grace drew as a child on the wall in her Fayetteville house.

Mike gave the army officers directions and then called our house. Dale and Leo were upstairs when the phone rang. I had left my spot on the stairs and was downstairs in the kitchen. I picked up the receiver and as soon as I heard Mike's voice, I told him to call Dale's cell phone. I wanted to keep the home line free in case Kimberly or someone from Ft. Bragg called.

Mike called Dale's cell phone and tried to stay calm, but he couldn't keep his voice from cracking. Dale knew something was very wrong. Mike took a deep breath and said what he had to say:

"Some army officers were at the old house and are on their way over."

"Mike, no," was all Dale could say.

"I'm so sorry," Mike replied.

"Leo, it was her," Dale said as he put the cell phone down. "I've got to go downstairs and tell Ann."

Dale looked at Leo. Leo looked at Dale. Leo felt as helpless as a man can feel. He had lost one of the people he loved most in the world. It was more than losing a best friend. It was like losing a sister. He could hardly bear watching her parents, whom he also loved, endure such unspeakable pain. Dale and Leo hugged, blinking back tears and trying to maintain some degree of composure.

I was seated in a chair when Dale came down the stairs. He knelt beside me and took my hand in his. His face was ashen.

"Mom, it's her."

We just held each other for a minute, and then I pushed him away.

"I've got to make some calls."

I dialed Sarita Hinkie first. I'd already called her something like fifteen times during the day to pour out my heart and my fears. Then I called family. I wanted my sisters and Dale's sister to hear it from me, not on the news.

We were waiting in the driveway when the gray van with government tags pulled up about fifteen minutes later. It was 4:20 PM, more than eight hours after I'd first learned a helicopter was down. It was almost exactly twelve hours after Kimberly had died.

We were both in shock. I was trying to keep Dale calm. He was consumed with anger, an anger he's said he's never felt before or since, not at the officers but at the enemy who had shot Kimberly's helicopter down. Dale's legs gave way and he went to his knees in the driveway as the officers walked toward us.

The officers, a chaplain and a warrant officer, delivered their message and condolences and read a little proclamation. They asked if we had any questions.

"Why did it take so long to bring the news?" Dale asked.

They said they had to drive up from Ft. Gordon, Georgia. It was a holiday weekend, and army regulations require that one of the two officers in a notification party be of equal or higher rank than the deceased. Because Kimberly was a captain, it took some time to find officers of adequate rank, they said.

We went inside, and just as the chaplain asked if we wanted to pray, Mike Haggard walked in the kitchen door. He'd gotten in his car as soon as he'd hung up the phone. Mike, Leo, Dale and I held hands and the chaplain led us in prayer. When the officers left, I asked Dale, Leo and Mike to take down the nine-foot Christmas tree that filled our front study.

I know this sounds crazy, but I remembered a visit Dale and I made one holiday season to the home of a friend who had died. The family was busy taking down Christmas decorations. Of course you don't want to be decorated for Christmas, I thought as I watched them. That just ran through my mind—you don't want to be decorated for Christmas.

It was busy work for numb minds, and more bad news was coming.

Earlier in the day, my oldest sister, Frances, had seen an oncologist and learned she had colon cancer. My sisters debated whether to tell me and add to my grief. They decided that waiting to tell me about Frances would cause me more hurt in the long run.

As the news about Kimberly spread, family and close friends began to arrive. It was ten at night before the house began to empty again. That's when the local FOX channel aired the news of Kimberly's death and the phone calls started. Thank goodness Leo was here. He answered the door and he answered the phone. He was a Godsend.

Before we went to bed, Dale and I made a pact. Kimberly would want us to speak out about the importance of the cause she fought and died for. She'd want us to tell everyone how strongly she believed in what she was doing. It wouldn't be easy. I'm a private person. So is Dale. Kimberly was, too. But her death was in the news, and we knew it was likely that we'd hear from reporters in the morning.

We didn't have to take the calls. That would be the easy thing to do. But Kimberly had fought—and given her life—for what she believed in. She could have chosen an easier life. She could have been here in Easley with us, teaching English and coaching tennis.

Telling her story honors her legacy and her sacrifice. It's the right thing to do. We made the pact, and I've never been sorry.

Donna Arnold, Kimberly's college tennis coach, hadn't checked her e-mail for a couple of days. She was at work at the Laurens YMCA—she'd left Presbyterian College—when she logged onto her e-mail and found a Christmas note from Kimberly. She showed it to one of the kids at the YMCA. There was a photograph of Kimberly's troops opening presents in a tent.

Later that night she was sitting on the sofa at home when her telephone rang. It was Ann Hampton.

"Kimberly's been in an accident."

Donna was up at the crack of dawn the next morning and on the road to Easley, a trip she would continue to make daily for several weeks to support Dale and Ann because she knew Kimberly was their life. She stayed strong for them, but when she came home at night, she cried.

Ken Porter, a close friend who worked with Dale and had known Kimberly since she was a toddler, was at the Peach Bowl game in Atlanta where Clemson was playing the University of Tennessee. He went to dinner after the game and got back to his hotel pretty late. He saw two phone messages and knew something was wrong. Before he could return the first call, the hotel room phone rang. It was a coworker who had been at the game and was already back in Easley. Mike Haggard had left a message about Kimberly on his home phone. He told Ken the news. Ken called Mike.

"Dale knew you were at the ball game having a good time and didn't want to ruin your evening," Mike told Ken. It was so like Dale, Ken thought. Dale had lost his only child and still was thinking of others.

Sarita Hinkie flew in from Oklahoma. She arrived around lunchtime Saturday. Her husband Ron had been away from home on business and Sam was in graduate school. They both flew in Sunday. The Hinkie's knew our grief. They'd lived with it since Sam's brother, Bill, died at age seventeen. Sarita took over the kitchen. It was a full time job. A stream of people filled the house offering condolences and, typical of Southerners at times like this, bringing food. As word spread, the house grew busier, with visitors from every aspect of Kimberly's life coming in and out pretty much from early morning until late at night for days. Sarita kept everyone laughing with funny stories about Kimberly and Sam growing up. She kept our hearts a little lighter.

Will's flight landed in Charleston, South Carolina, about two in the morning on Sunday. His brother Matt, who was stationed in Savannah, picked him up at the airport. They rested a few hours in Charleston and then drove to Easley. Will had never been to the new house, and it took a little driving around before he found us. The place was milling with people when he arrived in the middle of the afternoon. Dale and I took Will and Matt upstairs so we could be alone. We spent about an hour comparing what we knew about Kimberly's death. Will knew a bit more than the army notification party had told us, and he shared those details. In some ways it still didn't seem real. We were still in shock, but reality was starting to set in.

Will's parents arrived midweek. It was the first time we'd met them.

These certainly weren't the circumstances we'd expected for our first meeting. I'd imagined us meeting when Will and Kimberly were home from Iraq and planning the wedding. It wasn't supposed to be like this. But I was glad they came.

The office phone at Fort Hill started ringing early Monday morning and didn't stop for weeks. Dale's assistant, Sue Matthews, spoke with hundreds of callers every day. Dale and Ann wanted to hear about them all. Sue coordinated the food and other items going from the office to the house as employees rallied in support. Sue was amazed at how Dale and Ann made the effort to make every visitor feel welcome. They didn't just thank them for coming by. They took the time for real conversation.

Old friends and army buddies from around the world called. We wanted Kimberly's military friends coming to Easley for the funeral to have comfortable places to stay. Sue coordinated everything, like a travel agent of sorts, directing them to local motels.

Business and professional associates called with condolences. The mayor called. The local state senator came by twice and brought a former state governor with him on one of his visits. Senator Lindsey Graham called.

Rick Simmons, the county Veterans' Affairs Officer who had become friends with Kimberly in Afghanistan, was back home and brought us a Gold Star Banner, awarded to parents who have lost a child in war. I felt so sorry for him because I knew it was an emotional time for him as well, and I knew he put his duty and responsibility ahead of his personal feelings to come and do this for us.

"Here's their only child, a daughter," Rick thought to himself as he grieved for Kimberly and wondered at her parents' strength. "We're used to guys getting killed but were probably not used to our women coming home like this."

Local and regional news reporters called to get Kimberly's story. Rick suspected that Kimberly was the first American female pilot killed in action by the enemy, and confirmed it with military authorities. The local press reported it, and calls started coming in from journalists across the nation and overseas. ABC, NBC, CBS, and other major media sent reporters to Easley to interview us.

Public opinion on the war was changing. Kimberly was the 484th casualty of Operation Iraqi Freedom and negativity rose with the body count. We made it clear in every interview that we were proud of Kimberly, that she was doing what she believed in, and that we supported the president and U.S. troops. We were on an emotional roller coaster but we knew we were speaking for Kimberly. It was the only thing that kept us going.

Their lives were forever changed, but Dale and Ann weren't bitter about anything other than the enemy. Will was amazed at their strength. There was no way he could have talked with anybody at that point and here they were, facing the world and putting as much of a positive spin as they could on the loss. They wanted to focus on Kimberly and the positive things she'd done, and they were giving their all to shape the story in the way they knew Kimberly would want it told.

Then, in the midst of it all, Frances learned that the cancer had spread from her colon to her liver. I had lost my daughter. I was losing my sister. *How would I keep from losing my mind?*

Our first live national interview was with NBC newsman Bob Faw. He came to the house with a camera crew on Wednesday, January 7. Dale held my hand as we sat on a sofa in the upstairs den and looked into the camera and lights and talked about Kimberly. I was scared, I didn't want to cry, and it was hard to talk. Dale did most of the talking, but I managed to say a few words. The television camera zoomed in on my necklace, the gold helicopter charm, and I talked about how Kimberly had given it to me when she graduated from flight school. I didn't cry until the interview was over.

"She hated to see us cry," I told the television crew. "She did her job, and we did ours."

Then an amazing thing happened. The little miracles that still help us to make it through each day had begun.

The NBC crew and a local newspaper reporter were still at the house when our lake house neighbors, who periodically check our mailbox for us, arrived with a letter from Kimberly. She'd written it on November 23, after she had received a box of Christmas decorations I'd sent for the party.

"The singing snowmen will come back brown but we're going to have fun with them," she had written in the short note.

Our neighbors drove straight to Easley when they found her letter in the mailbox. After the stress and emotional drain of the television interview, it was a gift from God to hold the piece of paper Kimberly had held, and to read her neatly printed words.

"It's almost as if she planned it," Dale said, as we showed the letter to the reporters, who took more notes before they left.

The nature of Kimberly's death thrust us into the national spotlight and ripped away any veil of privacy that grieving families should have. We could have shut our door to the press. Sue could have told reporters we weren't taking calls. We felt Kimberly's letter was an affirmation that we were doing the right thing.

Kimberly's story was everywhere. The media couldn't get enough of America's newest hero, a small town girl with a captivating smile. She was a star athlete, a scholar, and an All-American girl who served in the 82nd Airborne, the army's All-American Division, a nickname given to the division in World War I because it had been formed with soldiers from every state in the country. Friends and strangers shared our loss as if it was their own. It's an understatement to say my heart was touched.

Making plans for Kimberly's funeral—on Saturday with full military honors—was surreal. But seeing the funeral arrangements on television made it all too real.

Dale's shoulders slumped as if he'd been shot when the funeral details flashed across the television screen. "You can talk about it all day long, but when you see it in writing, it hits home," said Ron Hinkie, who knew the pain of losing a child. "It's not ever going to go away. You don't want it to go away. But it will get better. Finally it's not the first thing you think about when you wake up in the morning."

The chill of loss is colder than the January day as Dale and I follow Kimberly's flag-draped coffin to her gravesite. *Photo by Bart Boatwright, courtesy of The Greenville News*

CHAPTER 13

A FLAG-DRAPED COFFIN

Visitation was at the Robinson Funeral Home in Easley the night before the funeral. Dale and I thought we'd schedule the visitation, a time when people come and pay their respects to the family, about an hour before the service, but the funeral director firmly suggested we do it the night before.

That turned out to be a good plan. We had no idea how many people would show up. It was a long night filled with surprises. Will and family members stood with us for five hours as family, friends, and strangers streamed through the receiving line, shedding tears and sharing condolences, hugs and support. It was amazing to see how many people shared in our daughter's life.

Lieutenant Colonel Terry Morgan came from Ft. Bragg with about a half dozen officers from the 82nd Airborne. They formed an honor guard by Kimberly's closed, flag-draped casket. People from across the country who had served with Kimberly and local folk who never knew her all came to pay their respects.

When Lieutenant Colonel Morgan arrived, he brought tragic news. Another member of Kimberly's unit, CWO2 Aaron Weaver, had died when a medevac helicopter he was riding in was shot down on January 8, less than a week after Kimberly's death. Aaron had survived Somalia and cancer. He had been told he couldn't go to Iraq with the unit because of the cancer treatments he needed, but he insisted on going anyway. He was on his way for a treatment when the helicopter was shot down.

Although our hearts were breaking with our loss, we realized that we weren't alone. Another family was going through the same thing, and our hearts went out to them as well.

We would later learn that even in death, Kimberly had given Aaron's younger brother, Ryan, an amazing gift he would never forget.

It's still difficult to talk about the funeral. The sanctuary at Rock Springs Baptist Church overflowed with mourners and emotion when Kimberly was laid to rest on January 10. It was a heroine's funeral with full military honors. Kimberly would have been embarrassed by the attention and the fuss.

Al Geiger, the Presbyterian College piper, strolled outside the sanctuary door in kilts and played the bagpipes. Haunting strains floated across the parking lot on a light breeze, accenting the already somber tone on the cold and overcast winter day, setting the tone before people even entered the church.

Red, white, and blue flowers and ribbons adorned the front of the church. Kimberly's senior portrait from college was on an easel next to her flag-draped coffin.

The portrait brought back memories for Kimberly's college friend Kelli Kirkland, who took a seat at the end of a pew with the Presbyterian College tennis team. Everyone on the team Kimberly played with was there, except two women who lived too far away to attend. They served as ushers and then sat together, with Donna Arnold, for the funeral. At visitation the night before, Kelli Kirkland kept looking at Kimberly's portrait, trying to grasp the fact that Kimberly was gone and remembering their time together:

> I was there when the picture was taken. I helped her pick out what she was going to wear for it. It was a khaki colored sleeveless linen dress. I think it had a little slit in the middle. I had probably worn it at some point. I wore a lot of her dresses.
>
> Visitation was the hardest time for me. At the funeral, with all these people coming into town and asking questions: "How are

you?" and "Are you ok?" and "Where are you at now?" all of those things overshadowed the day for me. The visitation was more of a personal time for me to deal with things.

Not being able to see her was hard. The fact that her body was in that box but her soul was not. It was like, 'wait a second, you were here yesterday and now you're not,' just the disbelief that comes from that. It was very overwhelming. I was just sitting there in front of her casket and looking at it and looking at her picture and trying to put it together.

The most intriguing thing to me was the person who accompanied the body. That's a whole job in the army, to be with her body until it's buried. She was one of my best friends and she died. That's awful, but she was also in the army, and she's a hero. All that began to hit when the army kind of took over her funeral with the full military thing.

Being there with all of the tennis team that day was special. It was a neat overlapping of all the people she had played with. I just kept thinking, "Kimberly, where are you? Everyone's here and we're all together and it's time to have a reunion and you're not here." I couldn't shake the feeling that Kimberly was going to walk in at any moment. I felt Kimberly's presence in the room.

Soldiers with the 82nd Airborne came by bus from Ft. Bragg and served as pallbearers. Wives of some of the soldiers who served with Kimberly and were still in Iraq came on the bus from Ft. Bragg as well. Other friends from Kimberly's military career found their way to Easley on their own, drawn to say farewell to a friend.

Matt Brady, who had taken Kimberly along on the medevac mission in Afghanistan, was working in a mobilization office in Oregon when he learned about Kimberly's death. He flew to Ft. Bragg and borrowed a friend's truck and drove to Easley to be at the funeral. He was driving across the Carolinas and realized he had no idea how to reach us because our phone number was unlisted. He checked into an Easley motel and left a message at the funeral home for me to call him on his cell phone.

"Kimberly would want you to be here," I said when I called him back, not realizing he was in town.

"I am here," Matt answered.

"No, Kimberly would want you to be here in Easley."

"I am here," Matt said.

I finally realized what he meant. I gave him directions to the house to be with the family.

Old friends from school days, family friends, and people from every corner of Kimberly's life filled the pews and balcony. Folding chairs were brought out to handle the overflow crowd as more than a thousand people filled the church. A place was reserved for newspaper and television reporters in a back corner of the sanctuary where they could set up cameras. Dale and I prepared a simple statement to be distributed to the press:

> We would like to express heartfelt gratitude to our family and friends, the local community, and members of the United States Army who have come forward to give comfort and assistance during last week.
>
> This outpouring of support has helped us immeasurably in dealing with the grief caused by the loss of our daughter Kimberly.
>
> We also want to convey the pride we feel in the job our daughter was doing serving our country and to express our deepest support for the men and women of our armed services and their families who continue to make sacrifices each and every day in protecting our freedom and the freedom of others around the world.

The organist played "Let There Be Peace on Earth," "America the Beautiful," and "My Country 'Tis of Thee," as soldiers with the 82nd Airborne filed into the choir loft. I walked in with Dale and Will on either side of me, and we took our places in the front pew.

The Rev. Dr. David Gallamore, pastor of the church, stepped to the lectern and began:

> Today we give honor to a great American. A lot of accolades have been given to her and rightfully so, and more are to come. The Bible says no greater love than this that a man or a woman lay down their life for a friend. That's exactly what Kimberly did for you and for me and this great country that we live in.

Sam read scripture from John 14:1–6 and 25–27:

Let not your heart be troubled: trust in God, and trust also in me. In my Father's house there are many mansions: if it were not so, I would have told you. I go to prepare a place for you. . . . This I have spoken while still with you, but the Counselor, the Holy Spirit whom the Father will send in my name, will teach you all things, and remind you of everything I said to you. Peace I leave with you, my peace I give to you: I do not give to you as the world gives. Do not let your heart be troubled, do not let it be afraid.

Two additional passages were read from the scripture: the well known passage from Ecclesiastes, "To every thing there is a season. . . . ," and the Sermon on the Mount from the Gospel of Matthew, ". . . Blessed are those who mourn for they will be comforted. . . . blessed are the peacemakers for they will be called children of God."

The organist played "God Bless America," and Dr. John V. Griffith, president of Presbyterian College, talked about Kimberly's love of a challenge and the kindness and generosity of spirit that were "always present in the remarkable smile that lit up her face."

The sun broke through the clouds outside and the light spilled through the sanctuary windows as he spoke:

I saw God's grace in Kimberly's life. It would be easy to say for such a competitive, seemingly driven person, that a huge list of accomplishments, and there were many, must have been for personal gain. Never once did I see her wear her many successes and achievements on her sleeve. She walked in to the classroom, the tennis court, and I imagine the battle field, with confidence, dignity, calm, and an eye for her fellow man. Her teammates, those in the army for whom she was responsible, her fellow students, all saw her as a natural leader.

Then it was Kimberly's college tennis coach Donna Arnold's turn to speak:

When Ann had asked if I would speak, I readily agreed but I wondered if I was up to the task. As my former tennis players gathered at the church that morning, I was overcome with emotion by their presence and was I afraid I'd choke up and let Ann and Dale down. But I could hear Kimberly's voice in my ear.

"You've got to be tough."

I walked to the front of the church and found the strength I needed. It was as if Kimberly was cheering me on from the side- lines, as I'd done for her on the tennis courts years before.

I talked about Kimberly's tennis career, her love of family and friends, how she loved Presbyterian College and how Presbyterian College loved her.

"Kimberly made me a better tennis coach. She pushed me as much as I pushed her," I said and told the quick step ladder story. The congregation laughed through their tears when I delivered the punch line, "We finally found something Kimberly couldn't do."

Lieutenant Colonel Morgan followed Donna, with a tribute to Kim- berly's service and her trademark smile and wink:

Each day Kimberly would greet every one of us with a simple smile and an eagerness to conquer the challenges that lay ahead. Mr. and Mrs. Hampton, your Kimberly was an outstanding paratrooper, confident, decisive, energetic. She truly enjoyed being a soldier and she truly enjoyed being a cavalryman, aviator and leading American sons and daughters as a commander. She answered a call to serve and defend our nation and our way of life. Just as she gave 100 percent to everything she did, she gave the ultimate sacrifice in this nation's fight against terrorism. Kimberly will be remembered as a commander who died leading her troops from the front and taking the fight to the enemy.

The bagpiper played *Amazing Grace,* and some Blue Star Mothers pre- sented me with a Gold Star banner, given to mothers whose children made the ultimate sacrifice for their country. One of the women, who also was a Gold Star mother and recently lost a son, clung to me and cried. I was amazed that she could be there and I knew she knew all of the emotions that I was feeling probably more so than any other person in the church. We received Kimberly's Bronze Star, Purple Heart, and The Air Medal. As we walked down the steps from the church, the soldiers lined up across the street, saluting as Kimberly's casket passed by. The tribute they paid her was awesome. The entire ceremony was somewhat surreal; we were just numb. We had to be. So many eyes were on us. The pain was so raw. We had to stay numb in order to make it through the day. The day Kimberly died was the hardest, but this was a close second.

The crowd followed the family out of the church into the afternoon chill with few words, climbing into their cars for the drive to Robinson Memorial Gardens about a mile away. The sides of the roads were lined with men, women, and children waving flags and saluting as the long funeral procession drove by. The feeling of Kimberly's presence that helped Donna deliver her speech remained as she slid behind the wheel of her car to drive to the grave site. It was as if Kimberly was sitting in the car next to her and she spoke out loud:

"Kimberly, you would not believe all the people who are here for you."

Little children who didn't know Kimberly waved American flags because they knew what she had done. World War II veterans who had lost limbs in another cause waited on the roadside in wheelchairs to salute their local hero as the hearse passed. It struck Donna that Kimberly now belonged to all of Easley and all of South Carolina. She represented the patriotic pride and family values prevalent in this place. Norman Rockwell couldn't have painted a more stirring small town scene as Kimberly was taken to her final resting place and her place in history.

The scene reminded Rick Simmons of a World War II movie when everyone came home a hero. Along the route he spotted his first grade teacher with her son, who was home on leave from active duty in the navy. She'd become assistant principal of McKissick Elementary in Easley, and children at the school had sent care packages to Kimberly during her time in Iraq.

Rick had been allowed to sit with Kimberly's unit in the church choir loft. At the cemetery he stood in formation with them as the caisson bearing Kimberly's flag-draped casket passed by. He felt humbled to be included with them and proud to have been Kimberly's friend.

RICK SIMMONS—

There were a lot of tears being shed by soldiers that day for their commander. Her death has great meaning. It was not in vain. She was doing exactly what she wanted to do. She's immortalized herself. A lot of people never have that opportunity.

A team of six English Shires, huge white draft horses, pulled the caisson through the cemetery. The only sound was the clip-clop of their hooves on the pavement. An outrider, the officer giving commands to the team, rode a seventh white English Shire. The honor guard from Ft. Bragg walked beside the caisson. A guidon bearer carried the red-and-white Darkhorse Troop guidon, which had been shipped back from Iraq for the funeral.

Another large draft horse, a black Percheron with an empty saddle was led behind the caisson to symbolize the fallen cavalry soldier. Spit-shined black riding boots were reversed in the stirrups and a sword was placed on the opposite side from where it would normally have been carried. The presence of the riderless horse was a high honor and distinction.

Before the last horse-mounted cavalry unit was disbanded in 1942, a fallen soldier's horse was draped in black, unless it was a black horse, and followed the casket. The military still uses a riderless horse for the funerals of higher ranking officers, full colonels and generals. But because the last mounted cavalry manual printed still called for a soldier's horse to follow the remains of all mounted personnel, and because Kimberly was a commander of a cavalry troop, the rules were bent for her funeral and she was buried in the old tradition in keeping with cavalry tradition.

Steve Riggs, who headed the caisson unit as a volunteer lieutenant colonel serving under South Carolina's adjutant general was impressed with the efforts of the soldiers from Ft. Bragg:

The 17th Cavalry really did a great job of bringing back two hundred years of U.S. Cavalry in its traditions. They thought it was important. They understood their heritage. They understood their mission. It was a joy to work with them.

Dale, Will, and I walked behind the riderless black horse. It was a cold, cold day, and by then we were numb physically as well as emotionally. About fifty family members and close friends were in a procession behind us that followed the caisson to the grave site. Dale had pinned Kimberly's Bronze Star to the left breast of his black overcoat, over his heart. His right arm was around my shoulders, and he held me tight as if willing us both to get through this. He held my left hand in his, and Will, on the other side of me, held my right hand. As we walked behind the casket, the sun came out from behind the clouds once again, as it did during the church service. As the hint of warmth brushed my cheeks, I felt like Kimberly was sending us a sign that she was fine and brighter days would come.

Hundreds of people filled the cemetery watching. There had been more than a thousand people in the church and even more were in the cemetery for the graveside military service. Active military and former soldiers lined the sides of the way saluting. Members of the American Legion and Veterans of Foreign Wars came from across the region and stood at attention. Governmental officials came to pay respects. Friends, acquaintances, local and national media, and other spectators watched from hillside vantage points as the procession slowly moved toward the Robinson Funeral Home canopy that had been erected over the gravesite. The sight of the grave and the reality it represented was almost too much to bear. I reminded myself that Kimberly had served a cause she deeply believed in. I was proud of her service and her courage, and grateful for all the people who had come to honor her. But I really just wanted to wake up from this as if it was all a dream. A bell tolled and the pallbearers lifted Kimberly's casket from the carriage and placed it at the front of the canopy. Dale, Will, Dale's mother, and I sat in the first four folding chairs under the funeral home canopy and held hands.

The pallbearers took the flag from the casket, folded it carefully into a triangle, and brought it to me. The officer who made the presentation made a short speech. He placed the folded flag in my arms and as he moved away I spoke saying, "I'd rather have Kimberly back instead." I had spoken softly, but aloud. I couldn't help myself. My words were barely audible. I don't know if the officer even heard. My words weren't meant for him. I was speaking to myself.

Dale and Will, on either side of me were having a tough time, also. Dale was focusing on staying numb. Will had attended other military funerals, although none as personally meaningful or big as this. He knew the sequence of events to come. As a soldier, he wanted to remain stone-faced and he tried his best. But when the bugler played Taps and the honor guard fired three volleys in perfect unison, he cried with the rest of us at the finality the two traditions represent.

When the formal military ceremony ended, everyone under the canopy placed yellow roses on the casket, yellow being the color of the U.S. Cavalry. Dale and I clung to each other and just stood there, frozen in grief, looking at the long stemmed roses and unaware of a crowd of photojournalists who snapped photos for the evening news and morning papers.

We remained at the gravesite for about an hour and a half as well wishers, from senators to strangers, offered condolences and reminisced and brought us back to the present. I shook off my sorrow as best I could and thanked them for coming.

Ken Porter carried a stack of box lunches over to a bus that soldiers were boarding for the five-hour trip back to Ft. Bragg. Dale had called him the day before the funeral and said he had a favor to ask:

"If I order some box lunches from the Honey Baked Ham is there any way you could pick those up" he asked me. "I can't imagine those folks riding all the way down here and not having anything to eat on the way back."

So as soon as the funeral was over I went over and picked up the lunches and brought them to the bus. Walking onto that bus with those meals and looking into the faces of those soldiers, and a lot of them had their spouses with them, it was like walking into a classroom of the brightest, most personable, best looking people that you could ever assemble together. These people are willing to die, to put their lives on the line every day. It just touched me, to walk in and be that close to them and be able to thank them for their service, to thank them for caring enough to come down that day. To think they are over there fighting so I can play golf or do whatever I want to do, it really got a hold of me that day. It was a bus full of "Kimberlys," men and women. They all had that personality and air of confidence about them. And they are all volunteers. No one drafted them. We take those people for granted and the sacrifices they make. To be around so many heroes like that, it was powerful.

As the members of the caisson unit loaded the horses into a trailer in a field at the edge of the cemetery and prepared to leave, a major general approached them with thanks and a request. He asked if they also would serve at Aaron Weaver's funeral in Tampa, Fla. The caisson unit readily agreed to do it. It was an honor to serve, and a way they could give thanks. As they discussed the arrangements, Sam Cooper, a member of the caisson unit, was struck by tears he saw streaming down the face of one of the officers with the major general.

SAM COOPER—
To see 82nd Airborne guys crying after the funeral, that told you how much they thought about her.

The sun had fallen low in the sky and the cemetery was nearly empty when Dale and I finally left. The core group of friends and family members returned to the house with us. We were exhausted. It was over.

The day after the funeral the house was still busy, but by the next day the activity began to wane. A few days after the funeral, Dale and I drove Will to Atlanta for his flight back to Ft. Campbell. I was so grateful he had been allowed to come and I hated to see him leave, especially knowing that the following day he would board a military plane and return to Iraq.

GLOBAL WAR ON TERRORISM
SEPTEMBER 11th, 2001
KIMBERLY NICOLE HAMPTON
1976-2004

OF
EASLEY

KILLED IN ACTION
JANUARY 2ND, 2004,
WEST OF BAGDAD, NEAR FALLUJAH, IRAQ

FIRST FEMALE COMBAT PILOT
SHOT DOWN AND KILLED
IN UNITED STATES MILITARY AVIATION HISTORY

FIRST FEMALE COMBAT CASUALTY
FROM
SOUTH CAROLINA AND THE COUNTY OF PICKENS

CAPTAIN KIMBERLY NICOLE HAMPTON WHILE SERVING AS COMMANDER (DARK HORSE 6) OF D TROOP, FIRST SQUADRON, 17TH CAVALRY, 82ND AIRBORNE DIVISION, WAS KILLED IN ACTION DURING OFFENSIVE OPERATIONS NEAR FALLUJAH, IRAQ AGAINST ARMED ENEMY INSURGENTS WHEN HER OH-58D KIOWA HELICOPTER SHE WAS PILOTING WAS HIT BY SURFACE-TO-AIR GROUND FIRE.

WITH HER BRILLIANT SMILE, SHE WAS THE FACE OF LIBERTY

Kimberly's name on the Wall of Valor in the Veterans' War Memorial Garden
at the Pickens County Courthouse.

CHAPTER 14

REDBIRDS, DRAGONFLIES, AND OTHER MIRACLES: EPILOGUE

A coincidence is just a small miracle where God chooses to remain anonymous.
—anonymous quote Kimberly copied into a journal
during her military years

DALE—

My heart ached. There was no way to fill the hole or stop the hurt. The sun was just rising over the trees when I woke up early one Saturday morning a few weeks after the funeral. The day was crystal clear, without a breath of wind. The sun was shining and it was just beginning to come up over the trees. I walked outside and decided to go for a run. I hadn't had the heart to run since Kimberly's death. Kimberly loved sunrises and sunsets. They were her favorite times of day. Now it was a reminder that I'd never share another sunrise with her, not on this earth, anyway. Now the streaks of color in the sky brought no joy, only the pain of loss. I hadn't run for several weeks and I knew I needed to do something to pick myself up. I reluctantly pulled on my running shoes and started down the street with a heavy heart. It was downhill to the end of the cul-de-sac, but when I turned around and started back up, the steep grade was too much for me. I was mentally and physically spent.

I was dying.

I said, "Dear Lord, I need some help," and I kept going. It was like I

191

could almost feel something behind me just pushing me. Before I knew it I was
at the top of the hill. I had this incredible feeling that Kimberly was with me.
The last time she was home we ran up at the lake. There were hills up there
and I remembered thinking to myself that I'm not going to let this kid run off
and leave me here. I got to thinking about that and it was almost like somebody
was giving me some help up that hill. I got so emotional when I got up to the
top. I kept going and I felt unbelievably good, but the hair on my arms was
standing on end and I just had this incredible feeling. It was almost like this
huge hole right here in the middle of my heart shrank a little. I just had a
strange feeling of comfort. I was crying and running and I ran all the way to
the highway and came back and it was just so sad she wasn't with me and I
was just so tired when I got back. I ran up the driveway at the end of the house
and was resting, standing bent over, resting my hands on my knees to catch my
breath.

   I still had tears streaming down my face. I heard a shrill sound. It was a
hawk—I know what a hawk sounds like—coming from behind me in the
woods across the street. When I heard it I raised up, and when I raised up, this
beautiful, beautiful cardinal lit in the tree right in front of me. The only thing
I could think of was, "My gosh, it's Kimberly." Why I felt that, I don't know.
I guess I was looking for something because I felt her, and the bird turned its
head and looked at me and flew off.

   Then I looked up and saw Ann. She had come downstairs and was standing
at the back door in her bathrobe. She came out, so I told her about it and we
had a good cry. It was a spiritual experience. I felt something I don't think I'd
ever felt before. It was as if Kimberly had sent a sign to say "I'm okay."

The full significance of the cardinal Dale saw didn't completely come to
light until about a month later when I was in Fayetteville packing up some
of Kimberly's belongings.

   At the end of January, Dale and I went to New York to be interviewed
live by Deborah Norville on MSNBC. We did it only because we felt it
was what Kimberly would have wanted. We never wanted to be spokes-
persons, but it was our way of honoring Kimberly's service and sacrifice
as well as the commitment and service of all of the other soldiers.

   When we returned from New York, I went to Fayetteville. I slowly
packed Kimberly's belongings into boxes. There were so many memories.

The wine glass Sean Jones had liberated from Sarducchi's, the Italian restaurant in Korea where he and Kimberly ate after her successful pilot-in-command flight, sat in a prominent place on a bookshelf. I wrapped it carefully. As I was packing Dale called. We'd gotten another television request. Dan Rather was going to be in Iraq and the network wanted some interviews to run while he was there. They wanted to talk with us. He had told them that I was in Fayetteville and couldn't be there, and they said they wanted to come to Fayettville and interview me there, at Kimberly's house. I didn't know how I was going to do it, alone without Dale there with me.

Then I came across a book titled *The Simple Abundant Journal of Gratitude* that Mike and Cathy Haggard had given Kimberly for graduation. I thumbed through a few pages. It didn't look like Kimberly had written in it, so I laid it down, planning to give it back to Mike and Cathy as a remembrance. Later I picked it up again and flipped through a few more pages and discovered that Kimberly had made entries in the journal for one month, while at Ft. Rucker in January 2002, just after returning from Korea. It just absolutely blew me away. There were numerous references to beautiful cardinals that came to feed in her yard and how much she enjoyed watching them. I thought about the cardinal that greeted Dale in the driveway after his run.

Kimberly had written in the journal about things for which she was grateful. I savored each word penned in her precise hand. Kimberly described the traditional New Year's meal of turnip greens and the feeling of safety while home with family for the holiday. She wrote about the comfort, peace and love she felt when I had visited her later in the month. The final entry, on January 31, praised my courage in resigning from my job. We had decided while she was home that I was going to retire and she was so excited about that. And it was great because I got to spend a lot more time with her than I would have.

Finding that journal was a gift. It did more than just get me through the television interview. Kimberly often expressed her feelings better in writing than verbally. It was comforting to read her words and to read about some of the simple things she was grateful for. It was not only just finding her handwriting, but what it said. The journal helped me through the ordeal of packing up the pieces of Kimberly's life.

I found another piece of solace as well. When I turned on the laptop at Kimberly's house an old Instant Message conversation we'd had a year earlier, when Kimberly was in Afghanistan, popped up on Yahoo Messenger:

December 7, 2002
Need to take a short little catnap —will be back in a bit. Hope you have fun at the party if I don't talk to you before you leave. Tell everyone hello for me. I love you!

The staff at Fort Hill Natural Gas encouraged Dale to take the time he needed for himself and to be with me before returning to work. They knew their jobs and how to keep the business running smoothly. When Dale did return to work, he and Sue Matthews were talking in his office when a cardinal landed on the second-floor window ledge. Dale had never seen any bird on that ledge before, not even a pigeon. Again, as on the day he ran, the redbird looked in at them, cocking its head, as if to say everything is okay. Cardinals became special to us, a symbol of hope for Dale in particular, but for me as well, and every sighting helped ease the ache in our hearts, easing the weight of loss one feather at a time.

The day Kimberly was killed, she was wearing the watch Will had given her the last time they were together, a few days after Christmas. After Kimberly died, Dale and I gave the watch to him. He left our house and was driving home from Easley when at 9:02 PM local time that night the alarm went off. Will did a quick calculation in his head. It was 5:02 in the morning Iraq time. It was the alarm she had set to get up that final morning in Iraq. Will hung the watch on his rear view mirror and left it there with the alarm still set, keeping a part of Kimberly with him. For us it's another of those small miracles that keep us going.

Although CWO2 Ryan Weaver never knew Kimberly, he will never forget her gift, and we are so grateful that he contacted us and shared his story. It was a gift to us as well. Ryan is the brother of Aaron Weaver, who was in Iraq with Kimberly and died a few days after she did. Lieutenant Colonel Terry Morgan brought us the news of Aaron's death when he arrived at Kimberly's visitation, and the South Carolina caisson unit that carried

Kimberly's casket to the grave site later took part in Aaron's funeral in Florida.

Ryan, a Black Hawk pilot, was stationed in Baghdad and flew a group of staff officers who knew Kimberly to her memorial service at Al Taqaddum. He was excited about making the flight because he'd get to see his brother Aaron, a Kiowa pilot stationed there with 1st Battalion, 17th Cavalry. Aaron was less than two years older than Ryan and they were close. Ryan hadn't seen his brother since October. He sent Aaron an Instant Message to say he was coming. Ryan could see the love people had for Kimberly in their grief, and his heart went out to her family. He thought to himself how he would never want to be the family back home. Ryan told us that he and Aaron both had tears in their eyes when the service ended. Aaron, a thirty-two-year-old survivor of the 1993 Mogandishu, Somalia, battle portrayed in the book and movie *Black Hawk Down*, and also a cancer survivor, told Ryan he'd seen too many brothers buried to Taps. When they parted, Aaron did something he'd never done before. Instead of shaking Ryan's hand, he gave him a hug.

That was the last day Ryan would spend with his brother. Aaron was riding in back of a Black Hawk—a medevac taking him to a doctor for a blood test—when the aircraft was shot down on January 8, two days after Kimberly's memorial service in Iraq.

Several days later, Ryan listened to Taps again, this time for Aaron. He thought about that last day he spent with his brother. His tears fell for two brave Kiowa pilots that day: his brother Aaron, and a woman who had brought them together one last time. It was an incredible gift.

About six weeks after Kimberly was killed, Jim Cornell was headed back to base from a night reconnaissance mission with Willy as his wingman flying with Adam Camarano, when they heard on the radio that some ground scouts were raiding a house nearby. They had plenty of gas, so they asked for permission to assist and flew to the location. It was a few miles from where Kimberly had been shot down. The area was gaining a nasty reputation for trouble. Both Jim and Willy have told us that they consider the events that ensued nothing less than miraculous. Here's how Jim tells it:

It was a night mission and a purely random situation. We were out doing one of the boring reconnaissance missions and we were on our way home. The mission was done. We had a ground element that was one of the troops in the squadron. They were doing a raid on a house. It was between us and the base. We still had some time that we could fly. When you are in a combat zone, you fly the mission that you are briefed and you go home. You don't go out joyriding. But we could deviate from that mission, with permission, if someone needed our help. Adam Camarano was on the radio checking in with the different units as we flew through their areas, and he got in touch with our ground staffs and found out they were not only on a mission, but it was pretty much in our route of flight to go back home. So he calls me up and says, "Hey, what do you think about going and helping the Alpha troop?"

"Call up the brigade, explain to them what's going on and see what they have to say."

The brigade says, "Yeah, go ahead. Help them out."

We go in and we're doing our standard checking out the perimeter, making sure no one is coming toward them, that kind of thing. This is about midnight on a really, really dark night. We find some guys that are about a hundred yards away digging a big hole, about the size of a foxhole. It was very suspicious. There was no reason for these guys to be out at midnight digging a hole. We flew in for a closer look.

They had some kind of a tube. We didn't know if it was a mortar tube or a shoulder-fired missile to shoot aircraft. It was in an area where we'd been having a lot of problems with aircraft being shot with missiles and stuff. It was about three miles from where Kimberly was shot down.

There was a set of power lines that ran down the road between where the bad guys were and where the good guys were. We discussed these power lines, we knew they were there. We went in on a gun run basically, without shooting to go in close and get a good look at what was going on to see if it was a target. We came off of that gun run and the guy that I was flying with said that he thought he saw a kid that was about ten-years-old or so with one of the three guys in this hole. Adam and Willy came in behind us and said they definitely saw the tube and were about 99 percent sure it was some sort of weapon.

Now we have a target. We have bad guys with a weapon in the vicinity of good guys. So we come off that run and we're circling back around and I'm talking to them."

"I really don't want to shoot a kid if I don't have to."

So as we're circling around, they said they saw the guys point the weapon at us. Well, now kid or no kid, we have to do something about this. So I came in on another gun run and I'm diving down toward the target. I was off line by a degree, enough that if it was daylight it would have been no big deal, I would have seen and been able to adjust with no problem. But it's so dark out there that I'm looking at where I thought the target was, right off my nose, but it wasn't right. The tree line was different. It just didn't look right.

I'm searching, I'm searching, I'm searching for this target, telling myself I know I'm holding this too long, I know I've got to pull out of this, and bam! I hit the wire.

They weren't industrial size wires, the kind you see in the States, pretty big ones, but they were big, about a hundred-feet tall. We had lost several people in Iraq from hitting wires and crashing and the crew not making it. I had about an eight inch gap between my searchlight on the nose of the aircraft that I had extended down and the bottom of the wire cutter (a metal wire cutter attached to the aircraft). Mike, the guy I was flying with at the time and I saw the wires at the same time. We were literally two or three feet from the wire when we saw it. Just instinctively I jerked back on the cyclic and brought the nose of the aircraft up and trapped the wire perfectly in that eight-inch gap and cut the wire with the wire cut-ter. It happened so fast you don't even have time to be scared. It was just intense. The helicopter was doing all kinds of weird things, bells and whistles going off, and then I realized the helicopter's still flying!

I had got a call off to Willy and Adam that we had just hit wires, so everybody's got their attention on us because they know the general result of wire strikes. I flew the aircraft about five hundred yards away and landed the aircraft and got out to check it out. Everything was fine.

I can't explain how it happened. I couldn't have planned it any better and I seriously doubt I could have repeated it. It couldn't have worked out any other way and Mike and I not crashed and died. That was the first incident where we really had collectively reflected that somebody was watching out for us.

Kimberly's name was added to the Wall of Valor in the Veterans' War Memorial Garden at the Pickens County Courthouse on March 26, 2004. This was the War Memorial Rick Simmons had created, the one he and Kimberly had talked about in Afghanistan after witnessing their first combat death. Rick had conceived and planned it as if it was his own child. He raised the money and oversaw the construction. Two years of his life went into it before its completion and dedication on Veterans Day in 1999. Rick couldn't get the promises he and Kimberly made in Afghanistan out of his mind, their pledge that if anything happened to either of them, the survivor would see that the other's name was put on the wall. Kimberly's name was the first added to the wall since it was built, and she was the first person killed in action that Rick personally knew. Dale and I realized that this was probably as hard for him as it was for us. These kinds of ceremonies always bring it all back. Rick threw himself into the planning and the program was superb. There was a Pickens County Council resolution honoring Kimberly, the Easley High band played, and the 17th Cavalry color guard from Ft. Bragg carried the American and other flags. County, state, and military dignitaries spoke. Poor Rick barely got through his speech. We could tell he was fighting to keep his emotions in check. Lieutenant Colonel Terry Morgan gave the keynote address and presented us with Kimberly's Global War on Terror Expeditionary Medal. Beneath the inscription listing the accomplishments of Kimberly's life and service are the words:

With her brilliant smile, she was the face of Liberty.

My eyes were raised skyward as a lone OH-58C Kiowa helicopter flew overhead at the end of the ceremony. I thought about my precious angel, somewhere up there in the heavens and surely watching. I wondered what she would think about all of the fuss.

In advance of the ceremony, I had silver helicopter charms made for my three sisters. They were replicas of the gold charm Kimberly gave me when she graduated from flight school.

The day before the ceremony, Martha was at the house with us, and I gave her the charms amid hugs and tears. Martha wore hers to the ceremony and put the necklaces on Louise and Frances there. Frances was in a wheelchair. She wasn't doing well, and I was concerned about her. She was weak from the cancer and failing quickly, but she wouldn't have missed the ceremony for the world. Frances died in June. She was buried wearing her necklace.

More recognition poured in. In April, the South Carolina branch of the United States Tennis Association announced that their annual "Most

Each Gold Star family placed a yellow rose during a memorial service at the 82nd Airborne Monument at Ft. Bragg to paratroopers who died in the Global War on Terrorism.

Improved Junior Girl Award," one of the state association's top awards, would be named for Kimberly and would become the "Kimberly Hampton Most Improved Junior Girl Award." On May 7, 2004, Kimberly was the first woman inducted into Presbyterian College's ROTC Hall of Fame. Her name joined the names of seven generals and twelve colonels on brass plaques displayed in the college's Military Science Department where she spent so much of her time while in college. In addition, an Easley High School Naval Junior ROTC award also was named for Kimberly.

The troop came home in April. In May we went up to Ft. Bragg for All-American Week and a memorial service. Even though we had met a lot of the guys at Kimberly's change of command, we didn't really have names to put together with them. But by the time we went up for All-American Week, we had heard from a lot of them and I knew a lot of the names. We had a get together at a restaurant. Initially Lieutenant Colonel Morgan, Lieutenant Colonel Viola, and Lieutenant Colonel Artman were there. They stayed for a few minutes, and then said, "We're going to leave you with the troop," which I thought was wonderful. We had about an hour with just us and Darkhorse troopers. We pulled chairs around and sat in a circle. They just talked. It was emotional. There were some tears, but they weren't ashamed of crying. It was so wonderful. There were some funny stories, too. They were so open. They opened their hearts. It shows how close they were. They were just like family. I wouldn't take anything for that experience.

Later, they were having a change of command and we were seated in the stands watching thousands of soldiers pass in review, when a dragonfly lit on the rope that separated us from the field. It lit on the rope right in front of us just as Kimberly's troop passed by and stayed there as they passed, as if watching for them with us. And then it flew away.

Like the cardinals that brought comfort to Dale, dragonflies became my talisman. From that day forward, I found a measure of peace in the little flying insects shaped so much like the gold helicopter Kimberly had given me to wear on my necklace. As time passed and healing began, more cardinals and more dragonflies seemed to fly in and out of our lives just when Dale and I needed a lift. It was as if God senses or knows that we're having some really tough times and sends these beautiful creatures to help give us comfort, and they do.

We consider these miracles. Kimberly was a miracle in the beginning. To even have had her, we were just blessed for twenty-seven wonderful years. I think God sees how we are hurting and he gave us these other miracles to help us. He gave us Kimberly, and she's gone, and he's given us these other things to help us find a way to deal with it, and that's the way we've learned to accept this thing.

Dale and I made a second trip to New York for *Glamour* magazine's Women of the Year award ceremony, when the magazine honored families of women killed in Iraq and Afghanistan. There was snow on the ground and it was freezing as we walked down the red carpet into the auditorium. Photographers were snapping pictures as people entered, and we felt out of place in the crowd of celebrities. But after we were with the other families who had lost daughters and sisters, the awkward feeling disappeared.

We sat with Rachel and Charity Witmer, sisters of Michelle Witmer, who was killed in Iraq on April 9, 2004, when her patrol was ambushed in the middle of the night. All three Witmer sisters served in the Army National Guard in Iraq. Michelle and Charity, twins, were deployed first, followed by Rachel, and local media had covered the story of the family with all three girls serving in Iraq. The story hit the national media, as Kimberly's had, after Michelle's death.

Rachel and Charity were beautiful in their formal dresses. I tried to imagine them in fatigues in a battlefield, but it was hard. The image didn't fit. They were as excited as college girls over the celebrity sightings at the ceremony, yet their grief was so evident. My heart ached for them.

Before we left New York, we went to Ground Zero, where the World Trade Towers had been. It was what Kimberly was fighting for. We felt an enormous connection with all those lost on Sept. 11, 2001, and all those who served in the resulting War on Terrorism. Kimberly had kept a patch in her pocket that was shaped like the twin towers and read "9-11 Never Forget." The patch was returned to us in the packet of personal belongings that Kimberly had with her when she died.

Kimberly's name was on the War Memorial, the flagpole in front of the Easley City Hall was dedicated in her memory, and Pickens County leaders also named a new multimillion dollar library being built in Easley in Kimberly's honor. We were guests of honor at a November 13, 2004 "Sneak Peek" at the new facility. It was officially dedicated on February 27, 2005. The day was overcast and cold. Many of Kimberly's friends and soldiers from Ft. Bragg came for the ribbon cutting. The ceremony was supposed to be outside, but it looked like it was about to rain any minute so it was moved indoors. There were speeches, and a cake in the shape of the library was cut and served with punch, and tour guides took small groups around the new library to show it off. In the midst of it all, the clouds cleared and the sun came out.

Adam Camarano was back in Iraq flying over Mosul on January 14, 2005, just over a year after Kimberly had been killed when a shot from an enemy on the ground hit his aircraft and set it on fire. There was no safe place to land, and Adam was painfully aware that the metal in the helicopter is very flammable once it starts to burn and it's pretty hard to stop at that point in time. Miraculously, he was able to fly the aircraft almost all the way back to the airfield to a safe place to land:

> I was able to fly the aircraft almost all the way back to the airfield to where I could find a safe place to land. I was able to land the aircraft and get myself and my pilot out of the aircraft in a safe area without the entire aircraft exploding or burning down. When the aircraft catch on fire they burn fairly quickly. I don't know if she had anything to do with that, but I was extremely lucky because it gave me enough time to get the aircraft to a safe location so that I wouldn't be forced down in the middle of an Iraqi city.
>
> We had the doors off. The fire was on the right side of the helicopter. My copilot was sitting in the right seat and I was in the left seat. The fire was so big on his side of the aircraft that he couldn't get out his door so he had to climb out my door after I got out.
>
> We were completely uninjured. I think the only thing I got was a bruise when I fell down a hill because it was muddy trying to run away.
>
> I felt that she was watching over all of our shoulders. That was the first big thing in our second rotation that happened to us. I felt she was there watching over our troop.

Two months later, on March 22, 2005, Jim and Willy also back in Iraq on the troop's second tour, found themselves in the biggest firefight of their careers up to that time. Jim was flying with CWO Charles Folk, and Willy was flying with Lt. Michael Hultquist. They were nearing the end of a routine shift when they heard a Mayday call that some American and Iraqi soldiers had been ambushed at Lake Tar Tar, in northwestern Iraq, north of Fallujah.

Although they were low on fuel, the two Kiowas went in, firing guns to give the ambushed troops cover.

The gunfire was intense. The American-Iraqi "friendlies" were outnumbered by foreign fighters: Jordanians, Syrians, and Egyptians who were armed to the teeth. The two Kiowas came in shooting and the enemy fired back. An RPG passed so close to Jim's aircraft that he could have reached out and grabbed it. Almost simultaneously the aircraft was hit at least twice. One bullet came up through the communications control panel, cutting off all communications, even the intercom between Jim and Chuck.

Willy and Mike's helicopter took at least thirteen rounds. One round hit Mike's armor side panel, which protected his torso. Willy looked at Mike whose eyes were glazed over, and his breathing was hard and heavy. Mike couldn't talk. Willy realized he needed to put the aircraft on the ground in the battle zone to get Mike to a medic.

He tried calling Jim, but got no answer. A shot went right above Mike's head and tore through the side of the aircraft. Willy landed and got to a medic. The bullet hadn't fully penetrated the side panel. Mike was ok, just stunned. They went back up.

They were out of bullets, out of gas, and both aircraft were badly torn up. They headed back to the base feeling lucky to be alive. It was fast and furious, but they'd done just enough to help the ambushed friendlies break contact with the enemy. They had walked into an ambush and there was no way they would have walked out without the Kiowas coming to the rescue. It was a miracle that the helicopters made it out with that many holes in them.

When they looked at the aircraft later, Jim realized that every one of about a half dozen bullets that went through the aircraft should have hit someone. One bullet went through the Plexiglas on the bottom and missed his foot by an inch. One bullet hit the top of the doorframe, barely missing Chuck's head, and went into a circuit panel. When Chuck sat in his seat that next day, they ran a braising rod through the bullet's path and it parted his hair.

They generally encountered poorly-trained enemy forces that raised their AK-47s into the air spraying bullets randomly. But the enemy they encountered at Lake Tar Tar was a well-trained military unit. Every bullet hole in each of the helicopters was centered on the cockpit and engine. Each bullet could have been fatal to the pilots, the aircraft, or both. Everything was a matter of inches. It was either pure luck or someone was watching over them. The four pilots later received the Distinguished Flying Cross for the mission. But getting the ground troops safely home meant more to the pilots than any medal.

There was no question in their minds that they had some help at Lake Tar Tar. Again, there was a feeling that someone was looking over their shoulders. They had no doubt that Darkhorse 6 still was flying with her troops.

On Sunday, April 4, 2005, a stretch of South Carolina 88 in front of our subdivision was named the Kimberly Hampton Memorial Highway. The stretch of road is in Anderson County, just south of the Pickens County line, and when an Anderson County councilman first proposed the idea, I wasn't sure if I could handle the daily reminder of highway signs I'd have to pass every time I left the house. Then I thought about what an honor it was for Kimberly and how comforting it could be to see Kimberly's name every day, and I agreed.

A ceremony was held at Mt. Pisgah Baptist Church, on the two-lane highway near the entrance to the subdivision that Sunday. The next day I went out and watched and took pictures as highway engineers erected the signs. I truly was happy I'd agreed to it. It was comforting to see Kimberly's name, and it made the new house, where Kimberly had never lived, seem more like home.

In June 2005, President George W. Bush gave a televised speech to the nation from Ft. Bragg and asked to meet with the Gold Star families who had lost loved ones in the war. Dale and I were among thirty-three families who met with the president that afternoon before his speech. Security was high and the post was like a ghost town that day. Jen Leidel, now Jen Ward, was our official escort. The families were gathered in a big open room for a buffet-style lunch of cold cuts, and then we were taken individually to small meeting rooms to wait for our chance to meet with the president.

The president received a short briefing before entering each room. We stood as he entered our room. He was taller than I thought he would be, and he certainly had a presence about him. He looked at Dale first, and then at me, and he held his arms out. The three of us hugged and cried as Andy Card, who was the president's chief of staff, and a photographer and a military liaison looked on.

The president said if he didn't know in his heart that he did the right thing in sending troops to Iraq that he couldn't live with the knowledge of the lives that were lost. We sat on a couch together and the president held my hand as we chatted. He wasn't hurried. He was totally focused on us. He and Dale chatted about natural gas exploration for a few minutes, and then the president looked at me and said, "You just heard more about that than you ever wanted to know."

"Yeah," I answered.

We told him that we support him.

"Kimberly is up there saying, 'You go, boy,' " I said.

The president laughed at that and then dropped his head. When he looked back up, I was surprised and moved to see tears glistening on his cheeks.

"I can't think about her tonight or I'll cry," he said.

The president took his handkerchief out three times during our meeting. He was sincere and comforting, and we felt that he was truly burdened by the loss of American lives, but we also could see his conviction that he had made the right decision for the country.

The president appeared unhurried, and gave us the time to say anything we wanted to say. As we continued to talk, we told the president about the Easley library that was named for Kimberly. "You know Mrs. Bush is a librarian," the president said

"Yes," we replied, telling him we were aware of that, and I reached for a small book I had brought as a gift for Mrs. Bush.

Water Bugs and Dragonflies, a small book by Doris Stickney, explains death

Dale and Ann meet with President George Bush.

to young children through the tale of a water bug that breaks through the surface of the water where all the bugs live and becomes a dragonfly. He wants to tell his friends, the other water bugs, what has happened, but now he can no longer go into the water. He realizes he will have to wait until his friends become dragonflies, too, and then they'll understand what happened to him. The book and the link to dragonflies had brought me solace and I wanted Mrs. Bush to have a copy.

As I handed the book to the president, he reached for a pen, thinking I wanted him to autograph it. I explained that it wasn't for an autograph; it was for Mrs. Bush. The president asked me to write a note in the book. I wrote an invitation inside the cover for Mrs. Bush to visit the Captain Kimberly Hampton Memorial Library. Andy Card reached out to take the book for Mrs. Bush and asked where Kimberly had gone to college. We talked about Presbyterian College and Andy Card said he knew the school. He had gone to the University of South Carolina and spent many weekends at Presbyterian College. It was a pleasant conversation.

It was only after our meeting ended and the president left the room that I realized I'd had the opportunity but neglected to get his autograph.

The meeting with the president was a high point, but the Fourth of July, the day after my birthday, was a rough day. I remembered Kimberly surprising me at the lake house on my birthday two years earlier and that happy day seemed so far away. The memory was like a ghost I couldn't hold onto. The grief was just too raw to bear. The prospect of marriage and the possibility of grandchildren had been in the air. Dale and I had plans drawn up for an addition to the small lake house to make room for a growing family. I hadn't been able to spend the night at the lake house since Kimberly's death. It was heart wrenching to think about what could have been.

I was having one of those bad days when I needed something. I walked to the front door and gazed out at a dragonfly garden ornament in a flower bed. Just then a tiny dragonfly landed on it to rest. I stood there and watched it, and it just sat there and sat there so I walked outside to get closer, and I thought that with the movement it would fly away. I walked to it and was right beside it for probably five minutes and the dragonfly sat there the whole time, and we kind of had a conversation. It stayed with me, telling me, as the cardinals told Dale, that everything is okay.

August seemed to come quickly, and Kimberly's twenty-ninth birthday was slightly less painful for us than her birthday the previous year because we were busy with the first annual Captain Kimberly Hampton Memorial Blood Drive. We cosponsored with The Blood Connection, an Upstate blood collection agency, in her memory.

"Who do you want to sing?" one of the workers at The Blood Connection asked me as they planned a small dedication ceremony to be held in the morning to kick off the blood drive.

"Lee Greenwood," I responded off the top of my head, "singing 'God Bless the USA.'"

I knew that getting the famous country singing star to Easley wasn't a possibility and I asked Kelli Kirkland to sing. Kimberly's two favorite hymns were "Great is Thy Faithfulness" and "How Great Thou Art." Kelli chose the first. She put absolutely everything she had into that song as she sang, and there wasn't a dry eye in the house. Dale spoke briefly, and when the ceremony was over I went to give blood.

It was something I had never done before. I didn't like needles and I was nervous about the prospect. The nurse was beginning the procedure, and I was bracing for the needle when the woman I'd planned the ceremony with ran in and said to turn up the radio.

"Do you hear that?'

Lee Greenwood was on the radio singing "God Bless the USA."

I figured the woman had called the radio station and requested the song, but she hadn't. It was just one of those coincidences—tiny miracles—just when I needed one.

The day was a huge success. The 552 units of blood collected would be a gift of life to potentially fifteen hundred to two thousand people. The library had been one of the collection points and people donated books as well as blood there. Donors brought bags of supplies to send to troops overseas as well. We had set a goal of 911 pints of blood going in but we knew it was extremely high and probably unattainable. The point was to encourage everyone that could to give and the blood bank personnel were thrilled with the response.

As we made plans to honor Kimberly with the blood drive, Cindy Sheehan, whose son also had died in Iraq, was making front page headlines with an antiwar vigil outside President Bush's Crawford, Texas ranch, demanding an audience with the president. On August 17, the day before the blood drive, a war protest rally was held in Greenville to support Sheehan. A photographer for a small northern Greenville County weekly newspaper photographed a woman at the rally holding a sign that read, "CPT K. N. Hampton." The newspaper identified the woman in the picture as "the mother of Captain Hampton" in the photograph that appeared on the front page with a story about the rally.

I hadn't been at the rally, and wouldn't have gone even if I'd known about it. I couldn't believe my eyes when I was shown the picture. I was furious. To be portrayed as someone going against everything Kimberly believed in and why she died brought back all the hurt of Kimberly's death with indescribable pain. I called the editor of the small paper and wrote a letter for him to publish, pouring out the emotion I'd held inside since Kimberly's death:

Letter to the Editor

On August 17, 2005, a war protest rally was held in Greenville which was sponsored by an organization called MoveOn. The organizers informed the media that family members of South Carolina fallen heroes would be the attendees. The rally was intended to be in support of the Cindy Sheehan vigil near President Bush's farm in Crawford, TX.

A lady who participated in the rally by holding a sign reading "CPT K. N. Hampton" was photographed by a reporter for your newspaper, and this photograph and an article about the assemblage appeared on the front page of the August 24, 2005 issue. The caption beneath the photograph identified the person in the photograph as the mother of Captain Hampton. I am the mother of Kimberly Hampton and I was not at the rally. Although I respect the right of anyone who chooses to protest President Bush's actions and our country's involvement in Iraq, I do not subscribe to the principles of the MoveOn organization . . . particularly their support of Ms. Sheehan.

We are dismayed, hurt and angry that someone would dishonor our daughter and our family by misrepresenting themselves in public as her mother. However, even more distressing to us is that this person's actions made it appear I am in opposition to the very things my daughter believed in and sacrificed her life for. Furthermore, although we are not journalists and have no authority as to how reporters should authenticate information that appears within the pages of their publications, it is clearly and disgustingly obvious your article contained a great deal of supposition as opposed to factual information for presentation as truth to the readers of your newspaper. I sincerely hope this is not a common occurrence.

Our daughter served her country by choice. She strived to be the best soldier, officer, commander and pilot possible. She knew that going to Iraq carried high risks, but she gladly accepted those risks. We supported her choice as do the overwhelming majority of families of those who serve our country in Iraq, Afghanistan and other troubled parts of our globe. We grieve daily for the loss of our only child and would gladly exchange places with her. Protesting the war is not the way she would want us to honor her, nor is it the way we choose to respect her sacrifice and that of all others who have given their lives . . . including Ms. Sheehan's son, SPC Casey Sheehan. Like all our troops in Iraq, Casey knew why he was there and he volunteered to go. Ms. Sheehan is intelligent enough to know that and should not need President Bush to tell her (again) what her son assuredly had already told her.

On August 18, Kimberly's 29th birthday, the day after the Move-On war protest rally in Greenville, our family co-sponsored with The Blood Connection the Captain Kimberly Hampton Memorial Blood Drive. On that day 552 units of blood were donated . . .the gift of life to potentially 1500–2000 people. We chose to remember Kimberly in a positive way which could help other people . . . not dishonor her by standing on a street in Greenville or in a field in Texas protesting the very thing that she so deeply believed in and died for.

At his request, we met with President Bush at Ft. Bragg recently and personally expressed our support for him and for our troops. There were 32 other families that day who also met privately with the president. We are not aware of anyone there that was sympathetic to the position recently taken by Ms. Sheehan. History will ultimately determine whether going to war was the right thing to do . . . and it may take years before the situation is fully resolved. Although there unfortunately will be other casualties, we are winning the war in Iraq. We must now finish the difficult job of winning the hearts and minds of the Iraqi people and this is being done bit-by-bit. To leave Iraq now would be a travesty. It would further expose the Iraqi people to the ravages of the minority insurgency. These people are, for the most part, foreigners, criminals and the dregs of Iraqi society who are fearful that a democratic government in the region will dilute their power and destroy their ability to dominate those who are unable to defend themselves.

We cannot fault the President for his convictions that he did the right thing by ridding the world of an extremely dangerous regime that fostered terrorism and inflicted much suffering and abuse upon its own people. Under Saddam, Iraq was a genuine threat to stability in the region, if not the world. Progress is being made in Iraq but there remains much more work yet to do before we are finished. We have many contacts in the military that substantiate the good things that are happening there. Unfortunately, many of the positive events are not divulged to the public by the mainstream media.

Our message to the MoveOn organization . . . parents, children, siblings and spouses have every right to protest in the name of their loved ones. We personally know of no one who has not been treated fairly or with great respect from anyone connected with the military and our government. Overall, the support for our troops and their families from the communities, state and the nation has been overwhelming. We urge everyone to continue supporting our troops and honor their sacrifices regardless of political persuasion or sentiment. It is demoralizing for those who protect our rights and freedoms at home and abroad to learn about the antics employed by people like Ms. Sheehan and organizations like MoveOn.

In closing, please reflect on this recently found poem.

It is the Soldier

It is the soldier, not the reporter,
Who has given us the freedom of the press.
It is the soldier, not the poet,
Who has given us freedom of speech.

It is the soldier, not the campus organizer,
Who has given us the freedom to demonstrate.
It is the soldier, not the lawyer,
Who has given us the right to a fair trial.

It is the soldier,
Who salutes the flag,
Who serves under the flag,
And whose coffin is draped in the flag,
Who allows the protester to burn the flag.
by Charles M. Province

Between the blood drive and the incident with the paper, the last two weeks of August had been an emotional roller coaster. August 31 was a couple of days away, the anniversary of those last goodbye hugs, I love you's, and pictures Dale took as he chased the cattle car to take a final picture of Kimberly as she deployed to Iraq two years earlier. The sad feelings were lingering more than usual for Dale, and he sat at his desk unable to shake them. It was only about eleven in the morning, but Dale needed to get away from his thoughts. He told Sue he was going to the bank. As he walked down the open staircase to the first floor atrium of the red brick office building, the receptionist called to him. Two men and a woman had just walked in and asked for him.

Dale had never seen them before and wondered what they wanted. They explained that they were in town for the Clemson-Texas A&M game the next day. One of the men was a Clemson graduate living in Helena, Montana. The other was a Texas A&M graduate living in Hawaii and the woman was his wife. The men had been in the marines together and met at least once a year for a Clemson or Texas A&M football game. Dale listened to their story, still wondering why they had come to his office.

They had read of Kimberly's death. The Clemson alumnus remembered that Easley was near Clemson and they decided to try to locate her family to offer their condolences. They went to the Easley City Hall and asked if anyone knew of Kimberly's family's whereabouts and were directed to Dale's office, a few blocks away. Dale was astonished. Had he left ten seconds earlier, he would have missed them. It was as if they had been sent to him to provide comfort during a rough time. Was it a coincidence? Dale didn't think so. Neither did I when he told me about it.

Willy Williamson can't put a finger on it and he can't explain it. He's convinced that Kimberly still flies with her troops because it's nothing short of a miracle that he survived a September 16, 2005 mission in Bakava, about thirty miles north of Baghdad. The enemy had mortared a forward operating base. The base had cleared the area and called the Kiowas because they were close. It was sunrise and the first rays of sunlight lit up the horizon as Willy and his copilot Scott Chachere arrived at the spot the mortars had been fired from. Willy was in the left seat and Scott was flying. Willy saw two men running from an open area as they approached.

Willy never flew with the clear visor of his helmet down, but for some reason he had put the face shield down that day. When Willy saw the men running, he snatched the controls and turned the helicopter around hard to the left to find the men as they ran into some trees. As the aircraft approached the tree line, Willy took a rifle round through his face shield. The visor deflected the round. It grazed Willy's hairline and went out the backside of his helmet. Scott deftly flew the aircraft to safety. Willie kept the helmet with the hole in it as a reminder that he and Scott had a protector on board that day.

But it was Scott's quick reaction, courage, and flying abilities that saved Willy's life that day. When Willy's wife, who also served in Iraq, gave birth to a son a year later, on September 4, 2006, they named him Maximus Chachere Williamson. Without Scott, and without their guardian angel, Willy would not have been around to have a baby.

They invited me to their baby shower. I traveled to Ft. Rucker, where they were stationed at the time, and held the baby. He'd been born early—he wasn't supposed to be at the shower. It was another of those bittersweet occasions. I was happy for them and honored to be remembered and included as an honorary grandma. But it also was a reminder that I'd never hold a grandchild that was truly my own, and I'd never see Kimberly's sweet face looking down at her own baby.

About three weeks before Christmas, nearly two years after Kimberly's death, Dale excitedly shared an e-mail with me that he had received from a Matthew Hampton, who knew Kimberly from her brief time at West Point. He hadn't known her well, but because they had the same name, after her death he ordered one of her KIA bracelets.

The day he sent the e-mail to Dale, he had been on patrol in Iraq when Kimberly's KIA bracelet got caught in the carrier of his machine gun. As he leaned down to clear the obstruction, a sniper round hit right above his head. He told us what happened:

> I ordered them from Ft. Lewis and the guy sent me two for some reason. I wore one and decided to put the other on the buttstock of the M240 Machine Gun. Well, in order to keep the weapon secured I used bungee cords while riding through Baghdad. . . . Well, the vehicle hit a bump and my flight suit sleeve got caught on the bracelet. I leaned down to free the bracelet and that's when the

round went right through the ammo can. If I had been sitting up, I would have caught it in the neck. Call it faith or divine intervention, it saved my life.

We read the e-mail in amazement. Something strange happened that day that saved someone's life. There was no question—a guardian angel was hard at work.

We corresponded with Matthew. On December 15, 2005, which was Election Day in Iraq, Matthew flew a flag in Kimberly's honor. The following February, after he returned to the States, he came to visit and gave us the flag, folded in a shadow box that also contained two photographs he took on that historic Election Day. One was of an Iraqi woman holding up her ink-stained finger that indicated she had voted. The other picture showed Matthew with the flag in Iraq. There was also a Bible verse:

Also I heard the voice of the Lord, saying, Whom shall I send, and who will go for us? Then said I, Here am I; send me.—Isaiah 6:8

These miraculous stories, these miraculous gifts that keep us going, just keep on coming and they do lighten our load.

During Thanksgiving week of 2005, Dale and I were in Jerusalem at the Wailing Wall, fulfilling our dream to visit the Holy Land. I was on the women's side and Dale was on the men's, and he had another of those amazing experiences. He watched as other people stuffed small notes of personal meaning into cracks in the wall, and then he walked forward and placed his own note, filled with thoughts of Kimberly, into a crack in the wall. Moments later a dove landed on the wall just above the note and rested there. To Dale, the resting dove was another winged messenger, like so many cardinals had been, bestowing a miracle of acknowledgment that his thoughts had been received.

On March 29, 2006, Dale and I were honored by the state Senate along with parents of other South Carolinians who had died in the war. Each family was presented the Palmetto Patriot award for their fallen hero. My heart went out to a woman whose son, a marine, had been killed in late

February, just a few weeks earlier. I admired her bravery in being there so soon after the loss. I didn't think I could have handled that environment so soon.

Tony Stout, another Upstate parent we knew, also was there. Tony was from Travelers Rest, just north of Greenville, and the first anniversary of the death of his daughter, Chrystal, was coming up on April 6. Specialist Chrystal Stout was twenty-three when a Chinook helicopter she was on crashed in Ghazni, Afghanistan. I knew the pain Tony must be feeling with the anniversary only a week away. It really doesn't get any easier, even twenty-seven months later, I reflected.

A few weeks later, in April 2006, Dale and I went to the ROTC commissioning ceremony at Presbyterian College and awarded the first annual Captain Kimberly Hampton ROTC Scholarship to a deserving rising senior in the program. The scholarship was given in Kimberly's name by a professional natural gas association and we knew how much it could mean to a young person. It was a scholarship offered by Presbyterian College in addition to the standard ROTC scholarship that brought Kimberly to Presbyterian. I thought about that day when Kimberly called me on the phone intermittently laughing and crying because she'd gotten her scholarship. The young man who received the scholarship seemed to be very humble, and we knew from what we had heard about him that he was a good student and a promising cadet. His parents and grandparents were there, watching proudly. It was another bittersweet day, filled with our own memories, but presenting him with the scholarship felt good.

We were back at Ft. Bragg for All-American Week and on May 26, 2006, the army named the 1st Squadron, 17th Cavalry headquarters building for Kimberly. Dale and I had agreed without hesitation when the army had contacted us to ask our permission. The cavalry was Kimberly's first love.

All-American Week is like a homecoming for the 82nd Airborne, and many retirees return for the occasion. It's a huge event leading up to Memorial Day Weekend at Ft. Bragg. The day started at 8:30 in the morning with a pass-and-review on the Pike Field Parade Ground. A group of Kiowas was leading an air-review fly-over, and Kimberly's friend Mac was in the lead aircraft as air-mission commander. Dale and I were looking up as we heard the familiar whir of the approaching helicopters. Then just before the helicopters came over the trees and into view, a dragonfly flew over us as if it was leading the aircraft in. Dale and I looked at each other and grinned, sharing our private joke instead of tears this day.

"She's giving him his orders," I told Dale. "She's telling him he better fly straight."

But it was impossible to hold back the tears as the day wore on. The dedication ceremony started at 2:00 PM. Dale had a tough time when he had to get up and speak to the large crowd, but somehow the strength came to him out of the blue. He was moved by the 82nd Airborne's wonderful tribute to Kimberly's sacrifice, and he knew this honor would ensure that her memory would never die. Literally hundreds of people approached Dale and me to speak with them during the course of the day, but it was a group of several young paratroopers who made the biggest impression. They said they didn't know Kimberly personally, but they had tears in their eyes as they thanked us for her sacrifice and spoke of the inspiration they received from her example.

As parents, their words were wonderful to hear. While we had wounds that would never heal, this helped tremendously. While the day was long and difficult and we went almost nonstop until seven that night, it was well worth the effort and the comfort we received chipped away a little bit more of the agony and further assured us that Kimberly's candle would glow forever.

The army had one more honor in store. On June 16, 2006, the Field Leaders Reaction Course, a training field at Ft. Lewis, Washington, was named for Kimberly. The field is part of the Warrior Forge, which all college ROTC students go through between their junior and senior years. We flew to Washington state for the dedication and were met by Will Braman, who traveled from Ft. Campbell, and Donovan McCartney, who was stationed at Ft. Lewis at the time. It was a joy to see them again and spend time with them. Will is family to us, and so many of the soldiers like Donovan, whom Kimberly served with and who have shared their experiences and their lives with us since her death, have become like a second family to us. Their generosity has made us rich in love.

Four separate training fields at Ft. Lewis were being dedicated to soldiers who had given their lives in Iraq and Afghanistan. As we visited two

Plaque on the 1st Battalion, 17th Cavalry Regiment, headquarters building at Ft. Bragg, North Carolina, which has been named for Kimberly.

of the fields where different courses were held, I could see why Kimberly loved it so much when she was there and came home from Advance Camp so pumped. Cadets crawled through the dirt and wound their way through and over obstacles. It was exactly what we'd seen Kimberly and Sam doing out in the woods as children, but it was also challenging mentally as well as physically. It was exactly the kind of thing that Kimberly loved.

In 2007, Rebecca Pepin, a new American citizen, put together a book *Faces of Freedom: Profiles of America's Fallen Heroes: Iraq and Afghanistan*. She felt this would be an appropriate way to say "thank you" to all those who serve. A fallen hero from each state was chosen, and volunteer writers and editors wrote a story about each. Kimberly was chosen to represent South Carolina,

There's been so much fanfare in the last few years to honor an humble woman who deserved the attention but would have been horrified and embarrassed by the fuss. This place was an important part of Kimberly's life and was a legacy she would have enjoyed. This is where a new group of young people is challenged every summer to fly in pursuit of their dreams, to live their lives with purpose, and to serve a nation Kimberly honored with her life.

Donovan McCartney, Dad, Mom and Will Braman at a training course named
for Kimberly at the ROTC Advance Camp, Ft. Lewis, Washington.

Dale and Ann cut the ribbon at new Pickens County Library headquarters
in Easley, named for Kimberly.

The love others shared for Kimberly has been a healing tonic for us. The pain of loss will never go away, but neither will the feeling that Kimberly still is with us, hovering like a dragonfly and cocking her head like a cardinal to let us know everything is okay. Perhaps the circle is closing. And perhaps somewhere there in the dust of an army training field, Kimberly is there watching and giving us a smile and a wink.

A view of Erbil, capital of Iraqi Kurdistan.

A roadside fruit and vegetable stand.

A street scene in Erbil.

A display of traditional Kurdish outfits at the Textile Museum in Erbil.

CHAPTER 15

IRAQ: 2010

I n early October, 2009, I received an invitation to a Hugs for Healing luncheon in Greenville from FUTURE, which stands for Families United Toward Universal Respect, where Gold Star and Blue Star mothers would meet with Iraqi women. The purpose of the event was to provide an environment in which everyone could share their personal stories of loss in order to promote healing. The program also included a Heroes Salute Ceremony, with speeches from VIPs, politicians, and dignitaries; attendees included the Iraqi Ambassador to the United States.

At first I wasn't sure that I wanted to meet Iraqi women, but the more Dale and I talked about it, the more I felt like going was the right thing to do. So I went, with no expectations at all, other than having lunch and seeing a field of flags, one of which would have Kimberly's picture attached to it. The luncheon started late because the Iraqi delegation, along with the FUTURE founders, Joan and Fareed Betros, and security personnel were delayed getting to Greenville's Donaldson Center. As I waited, I still wasn't sure that I should be there.

After a flurry of excitement surrounding their arrival died down and several speeches were delivered, all the ladies got together for hugs. Some of the Iraqi ladies couldn't speak English, but they could all say "Thank you" and "I'm sorry." We all cried and hugged and kissed and smiled, and they gave each of us gifts. That means the same in any language. I was glad I'd come. My healing had begun.

At the luncheon, some of the Iraqi ladies said, "Come to our country," and some of the Gold Star Moms said, "We want to come to your country." Joan immediately began planning the first of what hopefully will be many Hugs for Healing flights to Iraq. Initially I wasn't sure that I could emotionally make a trip like that. Dale, my rock, would not be able to go. The trip was only for mothers. I went with a few other mothers to Washington, D.C., to meet with politicians, State Department officials, an army general, and Iraqi Ambassador Samir Sumaidaie. We made lots of phone calls and sent letters. We hoped to find support for a 2010 visit to Baghdad, where we would meet with "Women for FUTURE—Iraq." Every door remained closed for us going to Baghdad, but another one opened for us to go to the Kurdistan region of northern Iraq. Personally, I was more comfortable with going there. A few months earlier I had been able to attend a presentation by Friends of Kurdistan founder Amy Ball, and she conveyed to us the love that the Kurds feel for the Americans, and their empathy for the Gold Star families. Travel to Baghdad would require military security at all times, and I cringed at the thought that a soldier could be attacked while protecting me. The Kurdish region, we learned, was relatively safe and has its own security forces: the Peshmerga. Dale didn't want me to go, but he told me that if I decided to go he would support me. He felt better knowing that I would not be in the Baghdad area, although just west of Baghdad is where Kimberly died.

After many months of planning, Joan and Fareed notified the interested mothers that a trip to Sulaymaniyah would take place in late September, and it was decision time for me. I was not afraid for my safety. I felt that the worst thing that could ever happen to me had already happened. Being away from home and family for ten days was something I was not sure I could handle. It was when I received a copy of the flight itinerary that I found my answer. The flight number entering Iraq was 818, Kimberly's birthday! I was going to Iraq.

I immediately began making plans, buying little gifts for the women and children in Iraq, deciding on clothing for the hot climate, paying for the trip and taking care of a multitude of other details. I was almost consumed with excitement. I knew that all would be well, and I felt like I had Kimberly's approval. I began to look forward to seeing the Iraqi ladies again, anticipated working with them on humanitarian projects for women's shelters and orphanages, and loved the idea of spending time with my fellow Gold Star Moms and the one Blue Star Mom who would be going with us. I really did not have any preconceived ideas about any benefits I would receive. My fears consisted of what would I eat for ten days . . . I'm a picky eater!

I told my minister about the trip and that I would be having a private memorial for Kimberly on Iraqi soil and he offered to help me. His support was an important part of my preparation and our talks often sustained me in the days leading up to the trip. He also planned a special service at church the Sunday before I left. The congregation surrounded me with powerful prayers and presented me with a prayer shawl that the church knitters had made. I wore a special prayer bracelet with prayer dots, which served as a constant reminder for me to pray. I truly experienced what it means to "pray without ceasing."

We left on September 23, 2010. Saying goodbye to Dale at the Greenville-Spartanburg International Airport was a bit emotional. I knew I would miss him and his comfort. I would have loved for him to be with me. But even if husbands had been allowed, he never could have handled all the women! I laughed at the thought.

After a short flight to Atlanta we met Doug and Kirk, who would be our security for the duration. Doug was a gentle giant of a man who could stop Iraqi traffic with just a look, and Kirk immediately became our "son." Three Utah Gold Star Moms joined us in Atlanta, bringing our group to a total of eighteen people: nine Gold Star Moms, one Blue Star Mom, two security personnel, two reporters and a photojournalist, a chaplain, and FUTURE cofounders Joan and Fareed. Joan presented all the moms with beautiful "star" pins, and also a journal in which to write down our thoughts and emotions. We were ready for our big adventure, having no idea of what was in front of us. We were filled with excitement, but we quickly snapped back to reality when Doug and Kirk gave our security briefing. Doug left no doubt in our minds that his mission was our safety, and not necessarily our feelings. Still, we found him to be as caring as anyone could possibly be, and he and Kirk kept us safe and happy.

After a long flight to Paris, our layover allowed time for some airport souvenir shopping and also a chance meeting with a beautiful Syrian lady who had spent some time in the United States. She asked me about the large group of Americans sitting together, and I cautiously gave a brief answer. As we continued our conversation I realized she wasn't a terrorist, just a very nice lady who recognized that we were a group on a mission. As I told her that we were nine Gold Star moms going to Iraq because our children died there, her eyes filled with tears. Amazingly she knew the meaning of "Gold Star," which is more than a lot of Americans know. I told her a little about our plans for humanitarian projects and that this was the inaugural Hugs for Healing flight. As we parted company she wanted to hug me, because just in our conversation she said that she had witnessed some healing in her own heart. Wow . . . little did I know how many times those feelings would be repeated over the next few days.

The flight from Paris to Amman, Jordan, was uneventful, and about half the previous flight time. We were met by a representative of the royal family who helped expedite our arrival and transportation to a local hotel. And the best part: I was able to get cell reception to call Dale, one of many calls I was able to make to him! He was so happy to hear from me, and it was also the first he'd heard that we had security with us. Oops, that was one detail I had previously failed to tell him; I could hear the relief in his voice. The hotel left a little to be desired, but it was a place to get a brief rest before our morning flight into Iraq.

Day Three was emotional as we boarded the plane for Iraq. We were tired, yet full of anticipation. We were still wearing basically the same clothes we left home in, but somehow that wasn't even important. I reflected on how Kimberly must have felt the day she flew into Iraq, almost exactly seven years earlier to the day. The flight number 818 reminded me again of Kimberly's birth date, so I knew she would be flying along with me. A few short weeks before she died she told me in an e-mail that she was with us in spirit always, and I have never felt that any stronger than when we crossed the border. I knew that as Kimberly went in on the helicopter she saw the same view of barren land with little vegetation. I thought about how she went in full of excitement, but then she didn't get to experience the pleasure of leaving. She didn't get to come home the way we'd hoped. I prayed for a time, holding tightly to my prayer shawl, holding onto Kimberly's picture. I looked at that beautiful smile and I felt like it was right for me to be there.

I looked at Penny, who was seated beside me, and wiped tears from her face. I held Elaine's hand over the seat where she was in front of me as she held onto her son Darius' picture. When we landed, through tears and hugs, Joan deplaned first and welcomed us to Iraq. Colleen dropped to her knees clutching her son Matthew's Marine blanket. For me this was not as emotional as crossing the border into Iraq. I was just open to whatever would happen. We all hugged again, we moms have a bond, an unbreakable bond, the bond created by shared grief of losing a child in Iraq.

Hugs for Healing . . . these are not empty words . . . they come with very real meaning. We entered the airport lobby and were greeted by familiar faces of some of the Iraqi moms who'd been in Greenville, as well as by new friends. The hugs began again, along with kisses now. There were at least two kisses and usually three for each hug. I've never been kissed so much in my life, and that was only the beginning. We were whisked away in buses, with police escort, to our hotel, where more Iraqi ladies were waiting to greet us. Each of us received a long stemmed red rose. We thought we'd be able to go to our rooms for a shower and a quick nap, but that was not so. We were told that we need to quickly change clothes and meet back in the lobby for lunch. From there we traveled to the offices of the Patriotic Union of Kurdistan (PUK) for a meeting with Kurdish political leader Mala Baxtyar. He thanked us for the service and sacrifice of our children in the liberation of Iraq. It was the first of many such messages we would receive.

Next we were treated to a traditional Kurdish meal and I began my ten-day diet of white rice, bread, a few occasional bites of chicken, bottled water, and an occasional Diet Coke. As I said, I'm picky. Others told me that the food was delicious, but I'm not adventurous in the food department. We were told that we should not drink anything but bottled water, and should not eat anything that had not been cooked or had been peeled. Kurdish tradition calls for a conversation period, with water and hot tea, then a lavish meal in a different room followed by fruit in another room. In addition to the political leaders at the luncheon, there were some family members of "martyrs" who expressed their appreciation for our visit and for our sacrifices. They expressed hope that our visit would help further strengthen the relationship between America and Iraq. A reporter with us questioned Baxtyar about the role of women in Iraq, and he replied that women receive equal pay with men, constitute 30 percent of Iraq's parliament and 52 percent of its university students. Already we were hearing things that we had never heard in the United States.

Every day we felt that nothing could be as emotional as the events so far, but every day we were proven wrong. On Day Four we went over to a huge, very modern conference center for the Women for Future leadership conference. There were hundreds of women and a few men there: Women for Future-Iraq, Anfal widows, Hero Ibrahim Ahmed, the petite first lady of Iraq and wife of President Jalal Talabani, Task Force Marne Deputy Commanding General Support Brig. Gen. Thomas Vandal, State Department officials, representatives from the Iraqi Martyrs Office, and our Hugs for Healing contingent.

First Lady Talabani spoke of her gratitude for American and Iraqi Forces working together to change the lives of her people and to rid the country of Saddam. Brigadier General Vandal recognized Amy's son, Cpl. Adam Galvez (USMC) who was killed by an IED, and my Kimberly. Yes, even though I'm filled with grief, I was very proud that her sacrifice is still being recognized.

I was particularly moved by the Anfal widows. These brave and tragic women are the living victims of Saddam Hussein's Anfal campaign of genocide, gendercide, and chemical warfare against the Kurds in 1988. He hated the Kurds and particularly wanted to get rid of as many males as possible. As a result, thousands of women were left to heal with no husband and usually several children. These widows now are revered for their sacrifice and what they withstood.

During the conference a video was shown of the 1988 chemical attack on Halabja, near the Iranian border. The Anfal widows, mostly sitting together, shed many tears, as did we all as we watched the chilling pictures. An estimated 178 thousand people were killed in some four thousand Kurdish villages. Their widows, dressed in black, have toiled and struggled for years to survive, and take care of their children. Their hardships are very evident in their faces. At the end of the program all the moms were invited onstage to receive flowers, and the widows came up to share hugs, kisses, and tears. There were no language barriers here. This grief is universal.

You could see the anguish and the heartache and the years of hard work in the Anfal widows' faces. Most of them wore the black gowns and

Ann sharing Kimberly's photo album with widow who lost 20 family members in one of Saddam's chemical attacks.

A Kurdish mother shows her grief to a Gold Star mother. *Courtesy of Cindy Hosea*

Happy children after receiving snacks.

Village children cautiously looking at laptop computer with Friends of Kurdistan's Amy Ball.

covered their heads in black. Their hands and what I could see of their arms under the sleeves of their gowns were as large and muscular as a man's because of the amount of manual labor that is part of their daily lives: farming, growing food, and tending to animals. Over and over they expressed their thanks and gratitude to the United States for ridding their country of Saddam Hussein. Many of the widows could not speak English, and they would touch their eyes as if crying to express their grief over our children who had died.

Those who could speak English gave horrifying accounts of how Saddam's bands came into their homes in the middle of the night and took children out of their beds and buried them alive while holding the mothers at gunpoint to keep them from trying to get to their children. Many of the victims were just put in mass graves. A lot of the graves weren't discovered until after Saddam was captured, and many victims still missing are presumed dead.

One day was set aside for community service. We went to a huge conference center and unpacked boxes sent by Salt Lake City-based Operation Give, a charitable organization started by CWO5 Paul Holton, who had served several tours in Iraq and was inspired by how excited Iraqi children were when he'd give them a toy or gift. Operation Give sent boxes and boxes of gifts and we also brought some gifts over ourselves. We assembled hygiene kits, packages of baby layette items, school items, hats, quilts, toys, dolls, and bead necklaces. Someone had brought a suitcase of soccer balls and books. We put together hundreds of gift bags. The Iraqi women, many of the Anfal widows and even the security guards helped out. We delivered packages to a women's hospital, a women's shelter, an orphanage, and a children's hospital.

As we put the hygiene kits together in zip-top plastic bags, I noticed that some of the Iraqi women didn't know how to close them. They had never seen these plastic bags that we all use at home in our kitchens and take for granted. It was a novelty for them.

The day when we held our individual memorial services for our children was a long awaited high point of our journey. It was a stiflingly hot day; the temperature must have been around a hundred degrees. We went to a beautiful resort in northern Iraq that was as nice as any upscale resort you'd see here in the United States The grounds, buildings, pools, and palm trees reminded me of a place in Hawaii where Dale and I spent our first Christmas after Kimberly died. It was perched above a large lake with a view of mountains across the water. First we had a nice luncheon. I asked our chaplain during the meal if he would give me communion later, following our individual memorial services, and he said he would offer communion for all who wanted to join in. We got some apple juice in little glasses and some bread to take with us for the communion.

First we held our individual memorials. Each mother was allowed to do whatever she wanted to do to honor and remember her child. My pastor and I had written the text for my memorial, and I chose to go away from the other mothers to deliver it. I asked two Iraqi women with whom I had formed particularly special bonds if they would like to go with me. One of the women had given me a necklace with a cross on it as a gift to let me know that even though she was Muslim she respected the fact that I was Christian. That meant so much to me. I told them I would be reading some scripture and asked if that would offend them, and they said no. They said they would love to go. A reporter with us asked if she could go too, and I said yes. The four of us went to a secluded area outdoors for Kimberly's memorial. I sat on a low wall, between the two Iraqi women. I think they cried even more than I did. They were very respectful and reverent, but they had their own memories. One woman's husband disappeared during the chemical raids and she can only assume he is dead. She was particularly emotional. She also has two daughters and I really connected with one of them during the workday at the conference center. I think she really was putting herself in my place and thinking about how she would feel losing a daughter, with the added sorrow of losing a husband. As they became emotional, I felt I had to be strong for them. I think I did pretty well. I don't think I totally lost my composure. When my reading was over, we shared a lot of hugs and tears. Then I went over to a small palm tree next to the building. The soil was rocky and I picked up a rock and used it to dig a shallow hole at the base of the palm. The ladies watched as I buried a little red glass heart with the word "Remember" etched in it.

I had spotted the glass heart and bought it some time before leaving Greenville for Iraq. I saw it while at a TAPS conference. TAPS is an acronym for Tragedy Assistance Program for Survivors, a military survivor group that other Gold Star mothers had recommended I attend. I went to the TAPS conference over Memorial Day weekend the year before I went to Iraq. I saw the little heart, just the right size to fit in the palm of my hand, and bought it while at the conference. I brought it home and put it in a dresser drawer. Every time I opened that drawer, there was that little heart. When I planned the trip to Iraq, I knew that I wanted to take it with me.

I also wanted the prayer shawl that had been knitted for me by members of my church with me for Kimberly's memorial. I couldn't actually wear it when I did Kimberly's memorial because of the extreme heat, but I had it with me. In fact, I carried it with me in my lap most of the time we were in Iraq. It felt like a real link to home and a link to God. Having it with me brought me great comfort.

After our individual memorial services, the chaplain offered communion to everyone who wished to partake. The communion was so moving and so peaceful. We had our apple juice and our bread, representing the blood and body of Christ, and a powerful reminder that we are all God's children and very much loved. We were all so spiritually in tune with one another that it was as if we were suspended in time. After the communion service we had a "Blessing of the Hands" ceremony. This was something new to me that I had never experienced in the past, but it certainly fit the time and place. We were in a big circle and the chaplain walked around each of us, holding each person's hands in his as he offered a special prayer or message with personal meaning to each of us.

None of the Iraqi women took part in communion or the blessing of the hands, but they were curious and watched with interest. After the blessing of the hands, all of us, Americans and Iraqis together, gathered in a large circle. Each woman took a turn and got up in front of the group to speak, say a prayer, a blessing or just share a few words. I had a prayer I had written before I left home and I started every morning with that prayer. When it was my turn to speak in the big circle, I recited the end of the prayer, asking a blessing on the land where we stood.

One of the other mothers read a part of a youth sermon her son gave at his church when he was sixteen. It was beautiful and spoke of peace and love. One mother sang a song that her son had liked when he was a little boy. Another mother sang the hymn "Amazing Grace." She told us that she often sang to her son when he was little, and "Amazing Grace" had been his favorite. While he was in Iraq, he told her that whenever he was in a firefight he hummed "Amazing Grace." She sang a verse, and then we all joined in. The Iraqi women didn't know the words, so for the last verse we all just sang the words "Praise God, praise God" all the way through and all of the Iraqi women joined in. That truly was a God moment. As we sang we were all one.

Next we each took a rock and built a little mound in the center of the circle where we sat. One mother took a rock she brought with her from her son's grave that had the word "Peace" written on it and added it to our rock formation. Another of the mothers had a crocheted angel, and placed it on top of the pile of rocks beside the peace rock.

It was an incredible day filled with a lot of healing. One mother had been extremely bitter, and as we traveled back to our hotel I asked how she was feeling. "I am finally at peace," she said. I understood completely. Although I had carried no ill will toward anyone, I had dealt with my own flood of emotions since the day Kimberly's aircraft was shot down and I, too, finally felt at peace.

The day before the memorial service we went to the little village of Halabja, close to the Iranian border, the site of Saddam's 1988 gas attacks where some five thousand people were killed within five minutes. All of the vegetation, everything, was wiped out at that time. Some vegetation has grown back, but it wasn't like it would have been. It killed the livestock and it killed the people. We saw mass graves where the dead had been buried. There were some survivors, and they are suffering from severe respiratory illnesses as they age. We met a couple of survivors from the gassing in 1988. They were children then and they do have severe respiratory problems. The Iranians came into the village and rescued the people who did not die immediately and took them back across the border six or seven miles away. There is a museum that has all of the people killed that day listed on the walls.

Seeing the devastation, seeing the results, seeing the barren land and seeing the museum that had depictions of what actually happened that day, brought a new understanding to all of our minds as to why the United States went into Iraq. People were so grateful to us that we did go in. We saw up close and personal the extent of the devastation that Saddam was capable of and what he did. The people there say he still had those chemicals when he was captured. We don't know. We'll probably never know for sure. I guess history will decide that. But the people there firmly believe that he did.

That was the information I needed to know that Kimberly didn't die in vain. There was a real purpose. We saw the heartache. That probably brought me the most reconciliation. I'm not over Kimberly's death, but I have a new understanding and a new peace that I didn't have before and probably never would have gotten if I had not seen the sights myself in Iraq.

Before we left, Mrs. Talabani, the first lady of Iraq , had her tailors measure each of us and make traditional Kurdish outfits for us to wear to her palace for dinner. Our new outfits were delivered to us just in time to dress for the occasion. They were made of four pieces. There were genie-style ankle length pants made of shiny fabric and simple round-neck sleeveless tunic tops that came down over the pants. The next layer was a filmy, colorful long gown that went on over our heads. The gowns had long flowing sleeves. Traditionally they take the ends of the sleeves and tie them at the back in a bow. You'd think they would be restrictive, but they were so wide there was no way you could wear the outfit without tying the sleeves. Then a little vest the same color as the undergarments and decorated with sequins and glitter goes over the gown to complete the outfit. All of our outfits were brightly colored. My outfit was orange. I had asked for red when we were being fitted but the woman measuring me shook her head no. So I had no idea what color I would get. When I saw the orange I thought about Clemson football games. All of the gowns were beautiful. The tailors tried to match the outfits to our hair and skin tones. Everyone had a different color: purple, lavender, green, teal, lime, and more. The men wore traditional outfits with turbans. This was an amazing evening, being whisked away to an ornate palace for dinner with the fancy clothes on. While it was ornate, it was not uncomfortable. Mrs. Talabani greeted us on the front steps when we arrived. Her dress was the same four-piece traditional style as ours but not as flashy. It was beige with a pinkish tint and more subdued. It fit her personality. She is outgoing in a quiet, elegant way.

We went into a large sitting room filled with paintings and statuary.

Chairs and sofas lined the walls, with small tables in between. Mrs. Talabani sat at the front of the room and welcomed us to sit beside her and talk. She posed for photographs with us all night long. She had her own photographers and many of the moms took their own pictures, too.

We moved from there to a large dining room decorated in a similar fashion with beautiful artwork on the walls. We were seated around two long tables and several smaller tables. One of the Gold Star mothers sat beside Mrs. Talabani at the dinner, and the first lady told her stories about hiding out from Saddam in the mountains in the late 1980s during the chemical rampages. Like the other meals we were served during our stay, the tables were filled with bowls and platters of food. There were a lot of rice dishes cooked with different meats and vegetables, tomatoes and chicken, and there were numerous variations of kabobs. If we asked what kind of meat it was, they would just say, "It is meat." I think some was lamb, and some looked like ground beef but didn't taste like it. It was probably ground lamb or something. I had one bite of it to see what it tasted like. It really was not bad, but I didn't want to do anything at all to risk upsetting my digestive system during the trip. The bread came in big flat rounds and we just pulled pieces off of it. There was bottled water and a selection of soft drinks.

After the dinner we went into a smoking room, where Mrs. Talabani gave each of us a beautiful crystal keepsake engraved with a tribute to our brave children. The inscription read, "Our eternal gratitude to the mothers who raised the bravest of children who dedicated their lives to the liberation of other nations." It was signed simply, "a mother" and engraved with her signature. In signing it with those words—a mother—I felt she was putting herself in our places and showing her compassion for the loss of our children because she's a mother also.

Then we went into another room where she had four pink-iced birthday cakes because it was the birthday of one of our moms, Colleen. She had wrapped a little gift of a necklace and earrings for Colleen and we all had cake. We sang "Happy Birthday" in English, Arabic, and Kurdish. Colleen's favorite color is pink and she wore a lot of pink, so I assume one of the Iraqi mothers with us must have told Mrs. Talabani in advance about the occasion and suggested pink icing on the cake.

We were treated like queens over there, and that was not because of anything we had done. It was because of what our children, our military and our country had done.

We arrived in New York on our return flight and it was time to say goodbye to the Utah moms and reporter and the others who were not going on to Greenville with us. As they were departing, one of the moms asked if we could sing "Amazing Grace" one more time. So the eighteen of us sang the hymn that had become our theme song together, there in the middle of LaGuardia Airport at about six o'clock as early-morning as travelers streamed around us as they rushed to catch their flights. When we finished singing, we kissed and hugged goodbye with gusto as onlookers stared. We had shared a life-changing experience and those stares didn't matter. "Amazing Grace" will forever be one of our strong bonds.

I returned home with a newfound peace. By the time we left we were all one big happy family. We fell in love with them and I think they loved us as much as we loved them. I've stayed in touch with some of the ladies through Facebook and e-mail. One of the women who had been with me for Kimberly's memorial—the woman with two daughters who'd lost her husband—went back to the resort where we'd held the memorials on Christmas Day and posted her own memorial remembering Kimberly's heroism on a wall. The memorial included two framed photographs of Kimberly with the words "Memorial of Kimberly," written in English and Kurdish and a gold wreath. She also placed a decorated Christmas tree by the memorial and e-mailed pictures of it to me. In August, 2011 I made another trip to Kurdistan with Amy Ball, the Friends of Kurdistan founder, and was able to see this memorial in person. My healing journey continued as I was able to visit with locals in small villages, and to hear the stories of their journeys to freedom from an oppressive regime.

The Iraqis and the Kurdish people we met are people just like we are. They want good lives, they want safety and happiness, and they want education for their children. Our children helped to pave the way for that to happen. Kimberly didn't die in vain. Although the loss still hurts and I still sometimes shed tears of grief, I am at peace.

Appendix

HON. JOE WILSON

OF SOUTH CAROLINA

IN THE HOUSE OF REPRESENTATIVES

Tuesday, September 20, 2011

Mr. WILSON of South Carolina. Mr. Speaker, I submit the following remarks from Mrs. Ann Hampton, who recently traveled to the Kurdish Region of Iraq. She is the proud Gold Star Mother of Captain Kimberly Hampton, who was killed in action on January 2, 2004, in Fallujah, Iraq.

"My recent trip to the Kurdistan Region of Iraq was everything I hoped it would be, and more! Traveling with another gold star mom and dad, a medically retired soldier, and the founder of the Friends of Kurdistan Foundation, the visit was filled with welcome events. We met several Kurdistan Regional Government officials, who all willingly gave us their undivided attention and treated us graciously. We were told over and over that their nation is our nation, their homes, our homes, and that we share the bonds of friendship forever. Their deep appreciation to the United States for liberating them from Saddam's tyrant regime knows no end. They said thanks.

"We visited hospitals, clinics, and villages in Kurdistan where progress is being made just as there are still hurdles ahead. We visited homes and were welcomed with open arms. We visited the home of a widow who lost 20 family members in one of the regime's chemical attacks. She fed us cantaloupe, bread and water, almost all she had. We visited a camp and were fed peaches and water, almost all they had.

"One very important thing Kurds and other Iraqis do have now is hope; hope for peace, security and maybe one day, prosperity. There was significant construction across Iraqi Kurdistan, which is a good sign that people have risen and taken charge of their freedoms, and serve also as role models to peoples in other countries in the Middle East and North Africa.

"I am very grateful for the opportunity to visit Kurdistan, and hope to go back again to continue my humanitarian work. Seeing and hearing the appreciation of the Kurdish people for the U.S. has made a tremendous impact on my healing, as a proud mother of an American soldier, Kimberly, killed in action liberating Iraq. The only way to move forward is by strengthening people-to-people links between Americans and Iraqis, in and out of government. The people of Kurdistan extended their hand to me, and I am grateful."

As the co-chairman of the Kurdish Regional Congressional Caucus I have visited the Region, and my oldest son led an Army National Guard convoy through the Region. We share the optimism of Mrs. Hampton that the liberated Kurdish Region of Iraq has a bright future of peace, security, and prosperity as a friend of America.

ACKNOWLEDGMENTS

W

e have so many people to thank for helping to tell Kimberly's story and for sharing their memories, their joys, and their tears. Their willingness made this book possible.

Our heartfelt thanks to all of those who served with Kimberly and who share her dedication to our nation: Adam Camarano, Maj. Andy Reiter, Col. Benny Steagall (USA Ret.), Maj. Brad Tinch, Crystal (Armour) Boring, CWO Donovan McCartney, Dave Gambrell, Command Sgt. Maj. Eric Pitkus, Sgt. Maj. Major Francisco Torres, Jason King, CWO James "Willy" Williamson (USA Ret.), Jen (Leidel) Boardman, Jen Williamson, CWO Jim Cornell, Col. James Viola, Cmd. Sgt. Maj. Joel Crawford, CWO John (Mac) MacElroy, CWO Lee Conley (USA Ret.), Leo Lesch, Maj. Manuel "Chief" Hernandez, Col. Matthew Brady, Matthew Hampton, Col. Mike Pyott, Col. Paul Bricker, Col. Rick Simmons, Robin Brown, CWO Ryan Weaver (USA Ret.), CWO Sean Jones, Col. Spencer Artman (USA Ret.), Col. Terry Morgan (USA Ret.), Maj. Travis McIntosh, and Lt. Col. Will Braman.

A special thank you to Lt. Gen. William B. Caldwell IV, who wrote the foreword, and to our literary agent, Dr. Gayle Wurst, of Princeton International Agency for the Arts, LLC, who came to this project early on, guided us through revisions, and was instrumental in bringing it to press.

We thank family and friends who shared their memories of Kimberly childhood and college years, who loved her and helped her become the person she was: Sam Hinkie, Alicia Limbaugh Tolbert, Cathy Whitman, Darah Huffman, Donna Arnold, Katherine Lathem Reid, Kelli Kirkland Mayfield, Lt. Col. Kirk Thomas (USA Ret.), Ken Porter, Lt. Col. Larry Mulhall (USA Ret.), Louise Williams, Martha Lewis, Mike Haggard, the late Col. Mike O'Kane (USA Ret.), Patsy Nabors, Ron Hinkie, Sarita Hinkie and Sue Matthews.

We thank those who helped us gain a sense of military tradition and history: Sam Cooper, Steve Riggs, Maj. Thomas Earnhardt and Lt. Col. Walt Pjetraj.

Special thanks for advice, expertise, technical support and friendship to Debbie Thrasher, Jimmy Mauldin, my father Gerald T. "Jerry" Simon, and my friend and mentor Dot Jackson, all of whom listened, read, and encouraged me along the way. And thank you, Dale and Ann, for the opportunity to tell Kimberly's story.

Ann touches Kimberly's name on monument at the dedication of the Global War on Terrorism monument.

. . . .

The royalties for this book benefit the
Captain Kimberly Hampton Memorial Foundation:
www.captainkimberlyhampton.org